D1563594

29-68

Twentieth Century
Political
Philosophy

Twentieth Century Political Philosophy

Donald Atwell Zoll
Arizona State University

PRENTICE-HALL, INC.

ENGLEWOOD CLIFFS, NEW JERSEY

Library of Congress Cataloging in Publication Data

ZOLL, DONALD ATWELL.
    Twentieth century political philosophy.

    Includes bibliographies.
    1. Political science—History. I. Title.
JA83.Z64   320.5   74-3161
ISBN 0-13-935049-7

© 1974 BY PRENTICE-HALL, INC., ENGLEWOOD CLIFFS, NEW JERSEY

Printed in the United States of America

10 9 8 7 6 5 4 3 2 1

PRENTICE-HALL INTERNATIONAL, INC., LONDON
PRENTICE-HALL OF AUSTRALIA, PTY. LTD., SYDNEY
PRENTICE-HALL OF CANADA, LTD., TORONTO
PRENTICE-HALL OF INDIA PRIVATE LIMITED, NEW DELHI
PRENTICE-HALL OF JAPAN, INC., TOKYO

FOR JOHN PATRICK WHITE

Table of Contents

FIVE

The Lodestone of Science: Neo-Positivism   71

SIX

The Common Man's Century: Popular Democracy   91

Preface

One need not use rash superlatives in order to describe the twentieth century as being "unusual." There is a distinct quality of lunacy about it. Even more than the nineteenth century, this is a century of the most striking and rudimentary extremes—high hopes and accomplishments are balanced by mad excesses, neo-barbarism, and the lively possibility that the life of the species might end, either as a result of some fiasco of human judgment and passion or as a result of the destruction of the very biological basis of man's existence. These paradoxes, tinged with a universal sense of dread and loss, make it difficult to separate with precision the intellectual currents of our age from the animadversions of a distraught humanity, a race of demimen, isolated from the verities that have sustained the inhabitants of so-called western culture over the past several centuries.

I take time to say this because the philosophical observer of the twentieth century finds himself in the same predicament as Nietzsche's "rope-dancer," striving, personally, to skip across the taut cable, while staring down into the abyss, cherishing the notion that what roils below is understandable and can be reduced to the pristine clarities of rational propositions. It may be a forlorn undertaking or, worse, the fascination with down-gazing analysis may dislodge the observer from his tenuous perch and he may tumble helplessly into the maelstrom he is seeking to traverse, little comforted, I would think, by Pascal's stinging observation that "men are so mad that not to be mad were a madness of itself."

I extend this thought as a sort of *caveat*. Historical distance or, more accurately, the absence of it, coupled with the peculiar pressures of contemporary existence, deny to the author of a book purporting to discuss twentieth century political and social ideas that austere and even leisurely perspective that can be exercised in regard to, say, the convolutions of the classical age or the Enlightenment. The author of such a book is a man caught in the box, hedged in by his accustomed scholarly rectitudes, but also enmeshed in the constrictions—I shall say even terrors—of the life of a contemporary man. Such an author must attempt to "make sense" of the political philosophy of this century, but he is never quite sure that he can or that what he proposes to dissect is, in fact, within the perimeters of reason. The temptation, often, is to question one's own rationality, but that, I submit, is not a vocational aberration of political philosophers, but the common condition of sensate human beings. The reader, too, may be asked to introspect.

If you, the reader, are willing to accept this predicament and with it the implicit sincerity of the author, then read away and we shall, together, see if we can negotiate the "tightrope over the abyss" and find more substance than shadow in the phantasmagoria of contemporary political ideas.

D.A.Z.

To the Instructor

This volume is not designed to encroach upon the obvious prerogatives of the instructor. The purpose of this book is to provide a brief over-arching panorama of political philosophy in the twentieth century, with some backward-looking references to the nineteenth, that will help unify and supplement what emphasis and specific works the instructor may choose to select. The length and organization of this text is constructed to augment whatever primary sources in twentieth century political thought the instructor may decide to use.

Additionally, the author has chosen, in the interests of readability, to dispense with conventional footnoting, but all works cited in the text, plus other appropriate references, will be found in the selected bibliography found at the end of each chapter. Also, a glossary of philosophical terms is included as an appendix, in preference to footnoting each term as it appears on the page. An index is also provided.

ONE

The Philosopher's Predicament

There is much talk today about "relevance." Often this word is more confusing than helpful, if only for the reason that one is entitled to an answer to the question, "Relevant to what?" Relevant to the "real world," you say? All right, but yours or mine? That may be a more serious problem than it appears to be at first glance. Can we be assured that we have a common intellectual world between us, let alone the ticklish epistemological issue of whether there is a common objective external world? Relevance may possibly be a wholly subjective matter.

This question arises because a popular charge leveled, contemporaneously, against philosophy is a lack of relevance. This is an unfair accusation if all that is implied is that philosophy fails to relate to some given individual's conception of his own personal realm of reality. But the more substantial thrust of the argument goes to the difference between *philosophy* and *ideology*, with the implicit suggestion that, somehow, ideology is superior because it intensifies "commitment" and enjoys a sort of rudimentary sincerity, presumably devoid of the skepticism and dispassion of philosophy.

Because in this century philosophy and ideology have, indeed, been in collision, it might be a good idea to differentiate their meanings. Two primary aspects of the nature of philosophy are that it is *tentative* and *critical;* in other words, it accepts nothing except on the basis of rigorous evidence or analysis, and it holds all propositions as being subject to refutation. Ideology, on the other hand, is a system of ideas that proceeds from certain propositions that must be accepted as immutable truths. In this sense, ideology is, in part, a "closed" system, requiring belief, even faith, in foundational premises. It is obvious enough, then, that philosophy does fall short of a total commitment and it remains invariably tentative. Of course, this may be an advantage *if* one assumes that there is merit in prudence or caution. The big difficulty with ideology is that you are required, by accepting it, to "put all your eggs in one basket," so to speak. If you are wrong, you are very wrong!

It must be conceded that, regarding philosophy and ideology, there are basic distinctions of "right" and "wrong" involved and that truth and error may be wholly subjective matters—something may be right or truthful simply because *I* hold that it is. The trouble with this formula, though, is that it is really functional only for lunatics and hermits. When we get to the business of communicating and espousing our convictions to others, something else seems to be required beyond our personal affirmations. Our contentions, to prevail, must be supported in some fashion by evidence, logical demonstration and inference, appeals to historical consistency, and so on. The risk in attempting to resolve problems by the counterposing of private truths leads to contests of passion, shouting matches or even, finally, force—"we measure out our truths in decibels" (with apologies to T. S. Eliot).

A part of the volatility of twentieth century political controversy arises from this enthusiasm for either ideological absolutism or the putative sovereignty of subjective revelation. One of the important functions of contemporary political philosophy may be simply to attempt to defuse, to some degree, the dangerous incendiary quality in the clash of social and personal value commitments.

I hope that I am not being too sanguine about the advantages of the philosophical perspective over the ideological or revelational orientation. It would be naive to assume that it is easy to preserve a philosophical detachment in the midst of the strenuous pressures of contemporary life. In any case, the "philosophical detachment" I speak of does not imply either retreat to the ivory tower or some opaque neutrality. Philosophical detachment may be a necessary intellectual posture, but it does not at all preclude individual commitments, moral, spiritual, aesthetic or political.

At base, the philosophical perspective is the denial of the sovereignty of the private ego, the acceptance of some standard of intellectual worth that transcends gratifications of the individual ego. Put another way, the philosophical perspective requires some additional justification for belief other than the intimations of individual desire—something is not necessarily true, philosophically speaking, just because you choose to believe it. At root, this is the idea that separates philosophy from magic.

Conventional definitions of philosophy have stressed the diverse elements in its viewpoint: logical, scientific, speculative; but, all in all, philosophy's most majestic contribution to the commonweal has been its *critical* function. Philosophy has been the disciplined "sieve" through which has poured the totality of man's ideational output, ultimately discarding, in the process, the untenable, the irrational, and the fantastic. It is not true that all the elementary issues stand as they did when Xenophanes of Colophon "took pen in hand." Philosophy is not an esoteric parlor-game, even if some "schools" in this century provoke that image. The critical function of philosophy has performed quite brilliantly across the vistas of the centuries. Some issues I take to be settled; I can assert that the existence of the "pineal gland," the moral justification for chattel slavery, and the tenability of the "divine right of kings," among other matters, are no longer at issue.

This vital critical role of philosophy can be sustained only if the philosophical perspective itself is preserved. There appear to be four major qualities in this perspective: the philosophical outlook is *skeptical, disciplined, speculative,* and *normative.*

The term "skeptical" is used in a broad sense to refer to a mood, a mental set, that refuses to take ideas at their face value and seeks an explanation for phenomena beyond the artifices of persuasion. It is this skeptical mood that divides *philosophers* (lovers of wisdom) from *philodoxers* (lovers of opinion).

The philosophical perspective also requires discipline, both of the mind and emotions and also of method and forms of investigation. The philosophical attitude is never very far removed from logic in its wider meaning. The philosophical perspective may not demand a narrow or formalistic rationalism, but it is never divorced from *reason*. Defenders of irrationalism, such as Nietzsche, for illustration, still seek to justify their premises by an appeal to reason. Such a commitment to reasoned discourse on the part of philosophers, this implicit discipline, separate their styles of argument from the sophistic devices of the demogogue.

Next, the philosophical perspective is invariably speculative, that is, it is always willing to entertain bold and imaginative explanations, hypotheses, alternatives that are not restricted by either the existing social mores or the explicit limitations of empirical science. It may seek to transcend "practical" limits and endeavor to posit the "ideal"; it may ponder alternatives that are *radical* in the true sense of that word: conceptions that imply an alteration of viewpoint at the fundamental levels.

Finally, the philosophic attitude is ultimately normative; that is, it recognizes the universality of the problem of value and does not try to avoid it. A given philosophical position may decide to reject a concept of value, but it will do so only after a confrontation with the problem of value—the problem of the allocation of premeditated priorities in the making of choices. In this sense, the philosophical perspective is humanistic; it is sensitive to the human predicament which is largely constituted by the perplexities involved in resolving questions of value.

These four qualities fuse into the singular way of looking at the world that is characteristic of the philosopher. In a manner of speaking, this outlook does suggest a certain partial detachment, if for no other reason than the philosopher's lessened interest in immediate phenomena and an increased curiosity regarding the ideas that propel phenomena. In politics, this suggests a division of labor between those who study the activity of politics and those who scrutinize or project the philosophical base of political activity. Both forms of political study require a perspective of their own, although the inherent qualities of these orientations, hopefully, are not mutually exclusive.

The century in which we live does not provide an optimum climate for the philosophical perspective. In any case, in any age, the philosopher is the product of his own cultural setting (which he can only partially transcend) and he, like any other man, is the target of influences and pressures that are generated by social circumstances. It is necessary, in a sense, that this be so, as the philosopher's task is, in part, recapitulative; that is, he is in the business of reframing and reconstituting elemental questions within the peculiar configurations of his epoch and ethos.

The position of the philosopher—more expressly the social philosopher—in our century is somewhat paradoxical: his social role, for a variety of reasons, is apt to be more detached and isolated from the arena of public decision-making than was the case in earlier centuries. Yet, at the same time, this contemporary age is one of exceptional ideational pressure, if for no other reason than the impact of the "communications revolution." We are simply flooded with "ideas" during a period of unusual historical urgency in which the issue of cultural and species survival is real and paramount.

Much has been said, too, about political "polarization," the inducement to "choose up sides" and wage ideological warfare. Philosophers are not immune from these influences, but in submitting to this temptation, the philosopher runs the risk of jettisoning the philosophical perspective and of failing to perpetuate the critical function of philosophy. This perspective, of course, does not demand that philosophers stand wholly aloof from the crucial issues of their times—and few political philosophers have done so—but it does suggest that philosophers must avoid the "total commitment" of the ideologist and that the advocacy of the philosopher proceed from a realization of the nature of his vocation. The argument has been made that the philosophic perspective is a luxury that no one can now afford and that one's contribution at the "barricades" is more imperative than the traditional philosophical rectitudes. There are two principal fallacies in this argument, however: (1) the "trial of arms" suggested by the image of the barricade is ultimately futile unless it features some expression of principle, a defense of values, such principles and values requiring the maintenance of the philosophic outlook; (2) perhaps such angry, doctrinaire confrontations, finally to be resolved by the brutality of force, can be avoided altogether if those qualities indigenous to the philosophical perspective can be given greater credence, their utilization granted a wider social scope.

THE SETTING

There are some characteristics that set the political thought of the twentieth century apart from its antecedents. In this connection, it may be appropriate to date the twentieth century, for practical purposes, from the beginning of the First World War in 1914. That date marks the shattering of one world and the introduction of another. A splendid picture of this pre-World War I world is provided by Barbara Tuchman in her book, *The Proud Tower*. It was a world predicated upon accustomed arrangements and tranquilities, based upon a century of substantial peace. It was, indeed, a century that commenced at the Congress of Vienna in 1815. Certainly widespread causes of unrest existed, both philosophical and social, but, all in all, the danger signs were overlooked as the cultures of Europe and America went about their conventional business, still propelled by the pervasive optimism of the nineteenth century. Such dissidents as Marx, Nietzsche, and Freud had said what they wished to say, but it was not generally assumed that these ideas would shake the edifice of the nineteenth century, an era exhibiting the presumed triumph of liberal reason.

When the house fell in, no one was prepared. Certainly no one was prepared for the sheer carnage of the First World War that left its grim imprint upon Europe. Those born after World War I have become, in a manner of speaking, inured to cataclysmic events; we have endured World War II, the atomic bomb, the Cold War, and revolutionary ferment. It is difficult, thereby, to fully gauge the impact of the gigantic struggle that commenced in 1914 upon the western mind. Intellectuals stood back in horror. The literature produced as a result of the First World War was far more poignant, fulsome, and volatile than anything nurtured by the Second World

War. The mass slaughter of the first Great War hinted of Armageddon, to say nothing of the fact that that war demolished the social systems of Europe—half a generation lay dead on the bloody fields of France and Belgium. In the wake of the war's ferocity came the Bolshevik Revolution in Russia, the rise of Fascism, and the unleashing of all manner of mass fears and frustrations.

The First Great War "marked" a generation of writers, from Max Scheler to F. Scott Fitzgerald. Intellectuals, such as Freud, Thomas Mann, and Andre Gide, recoiled in revulsion and began exploring a way out. Madison Grant, pondering the consequences of the war, spoke of the "passing of the great race"; T. S. Eliot proclaimed the existence of the "waste land." Their confidence shaken, the war stimulated among thinking men a new social literature, melancholic to bombastic, from *All Quiet on the Western Front* to *Mein Kampf*, reactions to the instabilities wrought by the conflict.

A primary effect was to discard a "philosophy as usual" approach in favor of a literature far less formally constituted, ranging from poetic outcry to political polemic. Rapid cultural change wedded to an understandable desire to avoid a recurrence of a mass war produced a sense of almost desperate urgency. Introduced, too, were exotic elements in western political thought: neo-barbaric irrationalism, assaults upon virtually immemorially-enshrined social institutions, and what Ortega y Gasset aptly called "the revolt of the masses."

These factors significantly affected the character of political philosophy in the post-World War I period, which fragmented into a baffling variety of forms and vehicles. No longer could the intellectual pulse of the age be found in the formal treatise; one was forced to examine a spectrum of literary activities, from poetry, plays, and novels to political speeches and manifestoes. The call to "action," stimulated by the Great War, meant a widening gap between the "philosophical perspective" and its collateral literature and the cries of anguish and ideological exhortation.

In addition, the period was one of intense scientific activity and accomplishment, perhaps motivated in part by the belief that science could bail people out of their difficulties. In any event, the political philosopher was frequently eclipsed in significance by the revelations of scientists, and profound contributions to social philosophy were indirectly produced by scientific inquiry. The search for meaning in twentieth century social thought would demand a new scientific sophistication, an ability to relate the postulates of science to the normative issues of political theory.

Yet another characteristic of post-World War I social philosophy and, indeed, philosophy in general, was the abandonment of serious efforts to produce "synthetic" philosophies: comprehensive, integrated explanatory and speculative systems. The "synthetic philosophy" may have been, with some exceptions, the casualty of the "knowledge explosion," that extraordinary amplification of empirical knowledge that often appeared to defy consolidation, if not communication. Political philosophers faced the predicament of a superabundance of knowledge (of a certain empirical sort) rather than the converse. This expansion of data also reduced the efficacy of intellectual communication—a traditional concern of philosophy —and created a widening chasm not only between "sciences" and "humanities," but also between the theoretician and the practitioner. Some philosophers arrived at the conclusion that their principal mission ought to be the clarification of language. Certainly how to cope with the inundations of data became a critical philosophical problem.

Certain philosophical movements turned to highly specialized and even esoteric preoccupations in the face of this difficulty, seeking to stake out a manageable territory for investigation and speculation. Other philosophies sought a new integration between philosophical activity and explicit human concerns, to the degree of often blurring a distinction between the philosophical and the ideological. Still others sought to model the philosophical enterprise upon the scientific one and unify the intellectual quest under the banner of Science.

These varied maneuvers had the effect of further removing philosophical work from the arena of affairs, particularly in the case of political philosophy, except insofar as political theory served as an apologia for specific political movements. Political philosophy was accused of "fiddling while Rome burns." Bona fide political philosophy was, in fact, caught in a bind: it sought to avoid being a pawn in the ideological struggle, while, at the same time, it did strive to affect the course of human events.

There was a real concern, especially in the post-World War II era, that political philosophy was a dying business. Its impact upon the public mind—and, indeed, upon the cerebral processes of statesmen—was seen as diminishing to the point of extinction. Three factors might be kept in mind, however, in making such an assessment: one, if political philosophy had become much less formalistic by the middle of the twentieth century, it is not consequently, valid to evaluate its health solely by an examination of its formal or academic products. Admitted that if "political philosophy" is to be defined as that which is produced by "political philosophers" (defined as those who professionally hold academic titles designating them as "political scientists" or "political theorists"), then the record is clearly questionable. However, much that is highly significant and pertinent to political philosophy has been forthcoming in the work of anthropologists, poets, theologians, lawyers, biologists, novelists, social critics, et al.

Further, a century that can produce thinkers of the quality of Santayana, Ortega, Voegelin, de Jouvenel, Arendt, Niebuhr, Strauss, Oakeshott, Mannheim, or Berlin can hardly be thought of as being destitute of political wisdom! The alleged atrophy of political philosophy may be in fact attributed to the failure of the culture to make adequate use of its "wise men," to a preference for what Jacob Burkhardt called the "terrible simplifiers" over the less emotionally titillating contributions of conscientious philosophers. Ours is an age of rapacious vanity, often cynically manipulated by opportunistic politicians, and such celebrations of popular prescience are rarely conducive to the recognition of philosophical significance and merit.

Two arch-enemies of philosophy are *hubris* and *evangelism*— and our contemporary culture prominently features both. Hubris, or presumptuous and ill-founded pride, is correctable by intellectual humility; evangelism (the secular variety) can be countered by a belated revival of reason. Both, unchecked, can abort the most salutary effects of philosophic endeavor.

One more substantial charge has been leveled against the vitality of political philosophy in this century. This is the accusation of moral indifference. Such an omnibus indictment is inaccurate and unfair, but there is a certain substance in the allegation, if more carefully delineated. A feature of some forms of political philosophy in this century is a radical separation of politics and ethics. I here refer not to the explicit advocacy of moral relativism or even to the contemporary manifestations of ethical nihilism, but to social thought that seeks to reject what could be called the axiological imperative—the requirement of facing up to the question of value as it relates to matters social and political.

My argument is not a neo-classical appeal for a political theory derivable from ethics, but, rather, the assertion that normative questions and political questions are finally inextricable, and that the political philosopher will have something to say about how to resolve value-dilemmas in the political realm.

While the phrase "the contemporary moral crisis" does smack of a cliché, this does not detract from its accuracy or pertinence. Ours is a time of moral troubles—troubles that not only haunt the regions of individual decision, but also that area sometimes referred to as the "civic ethic." It is the business, over the centuries, of political philosophers to address themselves to the matter of the civic ethic, to discourse upon the *nomos*—the sacred customs of the polity. It is probably true that post-World War I political philosophy has not addressed itself with adequate vigor to the discussion of this civic ethic.

In this sense, the demands, implicitly, of the body politic may have out-distanced political philosophy or a part thereof. The danger may well lie in the fact that the public, thus unsatisfied, might turn to other means for the resolution of their moral queries than the disinterested counsel of the philosophers.

Perhaps the most important issue confronting political and social philosophy in the last half of the twentieth century is the reconstitution of the human community. But such an enterprise invariably involves an understanding of the moral foundations of community. Political philosophy is thus presented, once more, with the elemental ethical dimension.

Even if major segments of political philosophy (and philosophy in general) tended to avoid the fundamental ethical problems, the mounting anxieties of the age expressed themselves in increasingly moralistic terms, particularly since the 1950s. It is one thing, of course, to discuss ethical issues and quite another to cast political and social preferences in moralistic language, and more of the latter is noticeable than the former. But the effect was to remove the moral dialogue, where it had lain dormant, from the philosophical confines, and place it in the more directly social and political arena.

Moral fervor and the recovery of a viable civic ethic upon which a humane politics might rest are not necessarily the same thing, and the contemporary political philosopher might wish to avoid the fate of Eric Hoffer's "true believer" and yet play a meaningful role in the general discourse regarding social ethics. It is a relatively simple thing for a philosopher to stoke the fires of moral intolerance—and many have in this century. A facile way of doing this is to find moral issues in human intercourse that are really not there at all. It is often astonishing, in retrospect, what have been some of the alleged "moral issues" over which men have been more than willing to kill each other—while obscuring, of course, the genuine ethical questions. In fact, perhaps we ought not to use the terms *morality* and *ethics* interchangeably. Possibly this tripartite scheme would be useful: (1) *custom*—to refer to social preferences such as tastes in speech, dress, or amusement; (2) *morality*—to refer to habitual associations and allocations of personal and social values, in part culturally determined; and (3) *ethics*—to refer to the attempt to frame rudimentary and universal "laws" or directives by which men and societies can regulate their conduct.

In the twentieth century, especially the second half of it, there has been a distinct blurring of the first two of these categories, custom and morality, and a manifest hesitancy to talk about the third, ethics. But morality—social or individual—requires, substantially, the participation of ethics unless custom or anti-custom is to be reified into morality. One concern of the social philosopher is to unscramble these categories and to place them in their proper relationship. And it could be hoped that this enterprise be not restricted to philosophers alone.

For the social philosopher, to become a political or ideological partisan does not assist him in this effort. It violates a reasonable intellectual division of labor, and yet immense pressures exist to persuade him to champion causes other than the rational examination of axiological alternatives. Two formidable forms of this pressure are what could be called the "decline of the West syndrome" and the "brave new world syndrome." Every thinking man or woman is affected by these to some degree.

The "decline of the West syndrome" expresses the view that, for a host of reasons, western civilization is at the brink of disaster of unprecedented magnitude—and the hour has passed for the luxury of philosophical reflection or an appeal to reason, and only defensive activism can be countenanced if civilization is to be rescued.

The "brave new world syndrome" is even more apocalyptic, if, in a sense, optimistic. A "golden age" awaits humankind if it stops idle intellectual dilettantism and presses forward—in some direction—in response to a subrational dialectic or the inexorable advance of theological ingenuity.

Both "syndromes" possess a modicum of truth. Western civilization is, indeed, in a serious predicament; a new age of amplified possibilities for human existence can be envisioned. But it is hard to believe that western civilization can be preserved by abandoning its principal attainments, particularly and foremost the rule of reason; nor can we anticipate a future "golden age" arrived at by replacing human sagacity with neo-primitivistic enthusiasms or the chilly functionings of machines or other organizational equivalents.

The response to the "crisis" would seem to be more philosophical sophistication, not less. It is not justifiable to write off this argument as a sort of philosophical bias, as a "trade" mystique of philosophers who can be so easily accused of cherishing the Platonic idea of the "good society" as one in which philosophers make all the decisions. Philosophical reflection is not the "hot-house" province of academics; it is a widely—if not wildly—open venture. It is a game anyone can play who is willing to accept the protocols involved.

We can revitalize political philosophy if we can accept this premise and couple it with Aristotle's conception that the term "political" is applicable to all aspects of human communal existence.

FOR ADDITIONAL READING

ARENDT, HANNAH, *The Human Condition: A Study of the Central Dilemmas Facing Modern Man.* New York: Anchor Books (Doubleday), 1959.

GERMINO, DANTE, *Beyond Ideology: The Revival of Political Theory.* New York: Harper & Row, 1967.

GILSON, ETIENNE, *The Unity of Philosophical Experience.* New York: Scribner's, 1937.

MABBOTT, J. D., *The State and the Citizen.* London: Hutchinson, 1967 (orig. pub. 1948).

MERLEAU-PONTY, MAURICE, *In Praise of Philosophy* (trans. by John Wild and J. M. Edie). Evanston: Northwestern University Press, 1963.

OPPENHEIM, FELIX E., *Moral Principles in Political Philosophy.* New York: Random House, 1958.

ORTEGA Y GASSET, JOSÉ, *What Is Philosophy?* (trans. by M. Adams). New York: Norton, 1960.

RAPHAEL, D. D., *Problems of Political Philsophy.* New York: Praeger, 1970.

SANTAYANA, GEORGE, *Three Philosophical Poets.* New York: Anchor Books (Doubleday), 1938 (orig. pub. 1910).

VOEGELIN, ERIC, *The New Science of Politics.* Chicago: University of Chicago Press, 1952.

WHITEHEAD, A. N., *Science and the Modern World* (Lowell Lectures, 1925). New York: Mentor Books (New American Library), 1956.

WOLIN, SHELDON, *Politics and Vision.* Boston: Little, Brown, 1960.

TWO

The Bridge of Vitalism

The Freudian Revolution

The two main philosophical currents in the last half of the nineteenth century, *idealism* and *utilitarianism,* were, each in its own way, flattering to human nature. Idealism, pushed to its limits by Hegel and his followers, did not have much enthusiasm for individual political liberty and man was surely not the measure of all things. However, man was seen as a projection of the Infinite, his essence and actualization attributable to the transcendental Absolute. The Hegelian dialectic—like all historical dialectics—was, after all, an "onward and upward" point of view. There was an aura of self-satisfaction, even pomposity, about Hegelianism and its offshoots, Left and Right, in the political taxonomy of the nineteenth century. The universe had been unlocked, presumably, by Hegel's key, and man, insofar as he appreciated the animadversions of the dialectic, could now proceed with admirable certainty and assurance, a mood which rather well matched the over-all *Zeitgeist* of the nineteenth century.

Utilitarianism, a home-grown British product that culminates in "classical liberalism," was no less flattering to the human ego or less fulsome in its implicit predictions regarding human progress. Being presumably empirical in spirit and method, the utilitarians-*cum*-liberals pushed individualism virtually to its limits, its ultimate apotheosis being the unrestrained mobilities of social Darwinism, presumed to be the free reign of "natural" conditions in human society. Man—individual man—became his own authority and judge, a state of affairs predicated not only on liberalism's view of human nature, but arising, too, from its moral relativism and persistent belief in the desirability of a restless, if dynamic, social pluralism.

Vastly different in metaphysical and ethical conviction, both idealism and classical liberalism shared one common viewpoint: men were highly educable. Men could be made malleable by social control in the Hegelian view or made better through educational efforts within an enhanced environment, coupled with "enlightened self-interest," in the outlook of classical liberalism. Indeed, the redeeming prospects of education, in the broad meaning of the word, characterized the spirit of the nineteenth century. Both idealism and classical liberalism laid great emphasis upon the supremacy of human reason—albeit they had differing versions of what constituted it. While only idealism was "rationalistic" in a technical, philosophic sense, classical liberalism was also broadly rationalistic in its reliance on cognitive human intelligence as the primary means of elucidating understanding. Indeed, classical liberalism's doctrine of human nature gave almost exclusive sovereignty of the conscious mind as the basis of its conception of self-interest.

Rationalism, in either form, led to the supposition that men were improvable by some educational enterprise, and, correspondingly, society could rest on a rational base, logistic or scientific.

Sooner or later, someone would challenge this hypothesis and when that rebuttal surfaced it took two forms: one was an assault upon the metaphysical foundations of idealism; the other was a critique of liberalism's underlying theory of mind. The first essentially anti-Hegelian reaction we will trace elsewhere (see chapter eight).

In its earliest inception, the attack on nineteenth century rationalism was primarily metaphysical and it represented a return to an ancient proposition: the search for the rudimentary substance of the universe. In simple terms, nineteenth century thought had chosen sides on the issue of what constituted the foundational category of existence. This difference of view represented a quite orthodox division between idealists, who insisted upon *mind* (i.e., ideas, mental processes, et al.) as the foundational category, and varieties of *materialism,* which advocated with equal vigor that the primary category was *matter.*

A third possibility was introduced by the emergence of *vitalism* which had as its progenitor that curious philosophical figure, Arthur Schopenhauer. The crux of Schopenhauer's metaphysical position was that the elemental universal category was neither mind nor matter, but psychic energy, which he designated by the term *Will.* Schopenhauer was not too precise about the nature of this universal Will, except that it was clear that it permeated all entities enjoying existence. He even alleged that the planets in their courses were driven by internal actualizations of the will! Schopenhauer's Will was an inexorable, crushing, all-consuming, blind "drive" that accounted for all activity of the natural realm, including human existence and behavior. It was, Schopenhauer concluded, useless to contest against the Will; human beings were simply victims of it, gaining only an occasional surcease from its cruel demands by aesthetic transport or the exercises of Oriental quietism. Life, in Schopenhauer's view, was a grim affair, as humans were helpless puppets of this rapacious universal Will.

Hardly anyone took Schopenhauer seriously. He was, after all, not a conventional philosopher. He was markedly contemptuous of the customary canons of philosophical scholarship and, moreover, he was unabashedly abusive to his philosophical colleagues. He was generally accorded the classification of "crackpot."

NIETZSCHE'S "BRIDGE" TO THE
PRESENT ERA

Schopenhauer's ideas did not go unnoticed by Friedrich Nietzsche, a rising philologist and social critic—as Nietzsche himself relates in his essay, "Schopenhauer as Educator." Nietzsche was to become, perhaps, the most eloquent voice condemning the nineteenth century, not only its philosophical orientations, but also its social institutions. The standard he ran up was that of *irrationalism* and in so doing he exerts an enormous influence on the thought of the twentieth century. Nietzsche's intellectual descendents in this century are legion and of all political and ideological stripes, although there are few, indeed, who announce a direct intellectual indebtedness to the author of *Thus Spake Zarathustra*.

Because it is our purpose to examine the political ideas of this century, it is beyond our scope to offer a detailed analysis of Nietzschean thought, but it is necessary to scrutinize those elements of it that provide a "bridge" into the current era.

Nietzsche was not explicitly a metaphysician. If it is possible to catalogue him, he is, at base, a moralist. Yet his ethical ideas, put forth in a number of his works, especially *The Geneology of Morals*, assume a metaphysic in part resembling that of Schopenhauer. For Nietzsche, too, the world is dominated by an on-going and imperious Will, but, unlike Schopenhauer's concept of it, this Will is glorious, liberating, triumphant, and the source of man's most elevated activity: creation. The knowledge of and recognition and response to the Will are not rational, not even intellectual. The awareness is of the instinctual motivations of the self. Man, for Nietzsche, as he embodies this Will is a magnificently predatory animal—a "great bird of prey"—and the natural hierarchy of human beings can be described in terms of the degrees of intensity with which the "will to power" realizes itself and dominates the attitudes of men.

This vitalistic world-view culminates in an attack upon the reigning theory of mind endorsed by nineteenth century liberalism. In short, man is neither a rational being nor did the crucial aspects of his mental life occur on the level of consciousness. The repression of the Will, the thwarting of the demands of the instinctual, sub-rational reservoir, becomes tantamount to illness. Health is to be described as "sublimation" (a Nietzschean term), the temporary satisfaction of the animalistic drives.

What Nietzsche had done was to lay the foundation for a counter-psychology (and, of course, by implication, a counter-ethic) against the remnants of the tabula rasa theory of mind. The inferences to be drawn from this irrationalistic proto-metaphysic and proto-psychology were variable, although in Nietzsche's own case they take the form of a radical critique of customary morality, the "transvaluation of value," a detestation of the state and political activities in general, an endorsement of the preeminence of the *ubermenschen* (the "over-men" who were naturally superior due to their fuller actualization of the "will to power"), the supremacy of creativity as a human value, the adulation of sensual excitation, a vigorous cosmopolitanism and a hatred of nationalism and, perhaps, the bitterest condemnation of Christianity in print, accusing it of the degeneration of western civilization.

It was not only Nietzsche's militant paganism that horrified his contemporaries. At base, four Nietzschean propositions collided with the most sacrosanct ideas of the nineteenth century:

1. The roots of existence were to be found in the lowest and most rudimentary levels of Being.
2. Men were dominated by irrational forces over which they could exercise only a tenuous (and, possibly, neurotic) control.
3. These irrational subterannean forces were essentially predatory and even bestial.
4. Men could never fully divorce themselves from their barbarian past; civilization was but a veneer over the engrams of a barbaric inheritance.

Nietzsche himself announced that his views were a "philosophy of life," a creed of creativity and affirmation, the positing of a new freedom, the renunciation of nihilism, and pointed toward a new and glorious age founded upon a revived naturalism and the ascendency of the over-men. But most of his contemporaries thought his vision of man to be dismal, brutal or sinister, or all three. By some, his philosophy was dismissed as the ravings of a madman. Women, particularly, found fault with his notion that females were biologically inferior and could serve no other good end than procreation and the comfort of the warrior. Nietzsche was portrayed as the arch-villain, the despoiler of religion and morals, the dangerous excoriator of liberal democracy. Clarence Darrow, for illustration, in his famed summation in the Leob-Leopold murder case, attempted to lessen the guilt of the slayers by intimating that their minds had been corrupted by reading Nietzsche!

But Nietzsche can hardly be dismissed as a philosophical aberration. His influence could be charted in the fuller development of vitalism and its off-shoot, *panpsychism*. Existentialism, in part, reveals his imprint. But nowhere was his impact so distinct as in the on-going development of depth or motive-torque psychology. Nietzsche's most direct heirs were Freud and Jung.

FREUD'S DEBT TO NIETZSCHE

Nietzsche laid no claim to being a scientist, not even in the *Wissenschaft* sense; he was a man of letters who triggered the imaginations of those more scientifically inclined. Sigmund Freud, who by training and temperamental disposition was a scientist, exercised, in turn, an enormous influence on philosophers and men of letters. How truly "scientific" were the conclusions of Freud is another matter, and it is doubtlessly true that, on occasion, he put on the mantle of the philosopher, in such works as *The Future of an Illusion* and *Civilization and Its Discontents*. But Freud viewed himself as a clinician and a scientifically-oriented inquirer. Initially, his purposes were far more restricted than Nietzsche's: he sought solutions to specific problems of human mental aberration. Freud never substantially departed from this view of his function, a conclusion suggested by the fact that he failed, by and large, to perceive the social and political implications inherent in his conception of the human personality.

Three primary differences separate a Nietzschean and a Freudian view of the human personality (metaphysics aside, a matter which Freud rather summarily dismisses):

1. The internal drives identified by Nietzsche are equally insistent in the Freudian view, but their unrestricted actualization is not deemed universally beneficial, the human subconscious being a repository of motivations, some of which are destructive, dangerous and socially intolerable. In the face of the prevailing mood of trust in cognitive process, Freud raises the spectre once again of innate human depravity, a sort of neo-Augustinian pessimism.

2. The balance effected which civilizes the primordial content of the subconscious is, for Nietzsche, subjective creative discipline, but for Freud it is a set of functional norms of social origin.

3. Nietzsche conceives the imperatives of the Will in broad terms culminating in a will to dominate. Freud, in turn, rests his conception of the subrational forces upon a predominantly sexual identification.

It must be assumed that whatever Freud's undisclosed convictions were regarding metaphysics (and we can only be certain of his anti-theistic preferences), he is, at base, a vitalist or, perhaps more accurately, a man who retained a naturalistic outlook on the universe, as befitted a presumably empirical scientist, who in the process of his investigations came to accept a view of nature as being permeated by vitalistic forces. In no sense is Freud simply a materialist who would reduce psychic process to physical function. Quite the contrary, the striking feature of his theory proclaimed the primacy of the psychic process over the physiological, a position for which he was much criticized by fellow scientists in his day and since.

Freud owed a considerable debt to Nietzsche, largely in providing a *Weltanschauung* from which to operate, besides the borrowing of some Nietzschean terminology. Freud makes mention of this himself in a number of places, including his *Autobiography,* but especially in *On the History of the Psychoanalytic Movement* where he comments regarding the influences of both Schopenhauer and Nietzsche. He remarks that Schopenhauer had worked out a theory of repression in advance of his own (in *The World as Will and Idea*) and of Nietzsche he writes:

> In later years I denied myself the great pleasure of reading Nietzsche's works, with the conscious motive of not wishing to be hindered in the working out of my psychoanalytic impressions by any preconceived ideas. I have, therefore, to be prepared—and am so gladly—to renounce all claim to priority in those many cases in which the laborious psychoanalytic insights can only confirm the insights intuitively won by the philosophers. (p. 939)

There is also no doubt that Freud was deeply impressed with the work of Charles Darwin (the *Origin of Species* appeared three years after Freud's birth), and his interest in Darwinian evolution perhaps lured him into a fascination for scientific investigation.

Some interpreters have understandably also detected a possible indebtedness to Dostoyevsky.

FREUD: AN OVERVIEW

Freud's biographers are agreed that from an early age he entertained no doubt regarding either his own genius or the inevitability of his making a contribution to human knowledge. He was spurred by a restless ambition—and it was reported that the young Freud took, as a boyhood hero, David Copperfield, a symbol of the fateful triumph of resolve over adversity. Freud was born in Freiberg in 1856 of Jewish parentage, an ethnic inheritance that frequently served as a focus for his thought. Initially not strongly motivated in the study of medicine, Freud excelled at the University of Vienna and finally became interested in neurology which led him to complete his medical degree in 1881. While on the staff of Vienna's General Hospital he became intrigued by the experiments of the French neurologist, Charcot, whom he visited in Paris in 1885, particularly in regard to the possibilities of hypnosis as a therapeutic tool in the treatment of hysteria. Continuing his own investigations (and later in collaboration with Josef Breuer), Freud began the development of the formative concept of psychoanalytic therapy, leading to the co-authored *Studies in Hysteria* in 1895. It provoked a spirited medical controversy.

Convinced of the value of the new technique (called *psychoanalysis* in the following year), he attempted a psychoanalytic investigation of his own subconscious in 1897, leading directly to his publication of *The Interpretation of Dreams* in 1900, considered by many to be his major work. Freud, by that time, had attracted a following (the beginnings of the Vienna Psychoanalytic Society trace to 1902) and he published *The Psychopathology of Everyday Life* in 1904. In 1908, the first international meeting for psychoanalytic studies convened at Salzburg with Freud surrounded by his early converts: Jung, Ferenczi, Stekel, Adler, and Riklin, among others. In the same year, Freud visited the United States on an invitation from G. Stanley Hall of Clark University and delivered five lectures (later to be published in 1910) and met the then-dying William James.

Freud was much disquieted by the disaffections occurring within the "psychoanalytic movement." Adler broke away in 1911 and Jung, his closest associate in many ways, was to follow suit a year later. Yet the important *Totem and Taboo* appeared in 1912. During the years of the First World War, Freud's most significant publication was his *Introductory Lectures on Psychoanalysis* (1916). The war, indeed, had a marked effect on Freud and broadened his intellectual interests. In the post-war period, he turned to more speculative works, such as *Beyond the Pleasure Principle* (1921); *The Ego and the Id* (1922); *The Future of an Illusion* (1927); and *Civilization and Its Discontents* (1929).

By 1934, psychoanalytic practitioners had fled Hitler's Germany and by 1938 with the invasion of Austria, Freud was forced to flee from his homeland, taking refuge in London. But Freud was suffering from a cancer that could not be arrested. On September 23, 1939, he died—only days after the commencement of the great holocaust of the Second World War.

THE FREUDIAN FRAMEWORK

Just what had Freud done to reshape men's self concepts and their relationships with other men? Freud himself gives a suggestion in his introductory lecture in *A General Introduction to Psychoanalysis*:

> The first of these displeasing propositions of psychoanalysis is this: that mental processes are essentially unconscious, and that those which are conscious are merely isolated acts and parts of the whole psychic entity. Now I must ask you to remember that, on the contrary, we are accustomed to identify the mental with the conscious. Consciousness appears to us positively the characteristic that defines mental life, and we regard psychology as the study of the content of consciousness. This even appears so evident that any contradiction of it seems obvious nonsense to us, and yet it is impossible for psychoanalysis to avoid this contradiction, or to accept the identity between the conscious and the psychic. The psychoanalytic definition of the mind is that it comprises processes of the nature of feeling,

thinking, and wishing, and it maintains that there are such things as unconscious thinking and unconscious wishing. . . . It seems like an empty wrangle over words to argue whether mental life is to be regarded as co-extensive with consciousness or whether it may be said to stretch beyond this limit, and yet I can assure you that the acceptance of unconscious mental processes represents a decisive step towards a new orientation in the world and in science. (pp. 22–23)

To this predominance of the unconscious mental processes, Freud joins a description of their content that discloses them as impulses, principally sexual in nature, that direct the behavior of the human organism. Freud's disclosures regarding the internal character of the unconscious (designated by him as the *id*) were not only controversial because of their fundamentally sexual composition. Freud's theory of the unconscious revived the question of the presence and nature of instinct as the formative element in human personality. That instinctual base contained motifs distinctly disturbing to an age accustomed to the complimentary and reformist attitudes concerning human behavior and mental processes developed by nineteenth century philosophy and social theory. Man was seen by Freud as being a creature driven by atavistic desires (the explicit character of which were but tenuously repressed by social inhibition), possessing a "latent aggressiveness," and filled with destructive urges, directed both against familial and social associates and the individual self.

If this was the basic nature of man, the problem for Freud—from the perspective of the diagnosis and treatment of mental disorder—was to determine how these primitive drives, these "memories of the primal horde," could be reconciled with the need to function in a social setting, a climate dominated in large part by cultural and historical restraints. While the demands of the id were primary (he introduces the term *libido* to refer to the sexual drives), it was impossible to imagine that these desires could be directly sublimated, that man, in sum, could live as an unrestrained animal. There were, as a matter of fact, certain deep-seated desires that were almost universally repressed by the configurations of cultures, such as incest and cannibalism. There need be, thought Freud, compensatory mechanisms that substantially meet the needs of libido and yet were socially acceptable forms of sublimation. In short, the human personality was comprised not only of the id, of unconscious instinctual drives, but also included control mechanisms that Freud identified with the conscious mind, the *ego*. The primary definition of optimum mental or emotional well-being was the absence of impairments to function—but that function was invariably within a social context.

The ego acted, then, as a form of control, of censorship, of the unacceptable primal wishes and drives of the id. That ego was, in part, socially conformed by the influences of family relationships and conditioning and the enculturation process undertaken by society; Freud refers to this facet of the ego as the *ego ideal* or, later, as the *super-ego*. Thus, while the basic composition of human nature is universal, the ego responded to the particularities of the explicit social development and situation.

This relationship between id and ego, between primal drives and social restraints, is highly complex, principally because experience never entails manifestations of "pure" libido (save, perhaps, in certain extreme cases of psychosis when the ego forces are drastically crippled and ineffective). There is no direct participation or penetration into the realm of the unconscious. The communication is a symbolic one: the raw demands of the id are filtered through ego censorship and converted into acceptable symbols which are causes, often, of anxiety and yet are not totally threatening to the ego or to the consciousness, containing, of course, its matrix of socially-engendered inhibitions.

But the problem for Freud was malfunction; the id and ego wrenched by some causation from a relationship that permitted, nominally speaking, personal and social functioning. This could only be analyzed in symbolic terms and Freud turned to a variety of techniques by which to "read" the content of the unconscious. Hypnotism was early discarded and in its place Freud resorted to the analysis of conditions when ego censorship was reduced, thus presenting a minimum of symbolic distortion. Among such techniques were "dream analysis," "free association," and the investigation of forms of more or less spontaneous expression, such as art, humor, and what he termed the "pathology of everyday life."

This enterprise could yield understanding of the nature and

blockage of libidinous energy, the failure of sublimation. But it was necessary to appreciate as well the composition of the ego, the forces arrayed against libido. This analysis must of necessity be essentially anthropological, and Freud turned to a number of sources of insight, including mythology and primitive social practices (as in his *Totem and Taboo*). Indeed, an entirely new anthropological orientation emerged from Freud's initiating work, some of which commenced during his own lifetime and under his direct influence, typified in the work of Geza Roheim, whose cultural premises rested on Freud's view of human nature. C. G. Jung pursued anthropological investigations stimulated by Freud, although proceeding from different assumptions regarding the basis and metamorphosis of personality. Jung's influence upon contemporary anthropology remains intensely significant.

Concern with the content of the id and the nature and operation of the ego were extremely suggestive in terms of diagnosis, delving into the possible causes of human personality malfunction, but was not in itself therapeutic. However, Freud became convinced that the sources of malfunction could be eliminated or alleviated by the process of the individual's acquiring an awareness and acceptance of the hitherto undisclosed forces and confrontations that underlay his inability to perform satisfactorily in terms of his own mental life or his social relationships. This was the foundational hypothesis upon which a new concept of treatment emerged, which Freud chose to call "psychoanalysis."

RAMIFICATIONS OF FREUDIAN THEORY

The world was startled by Freud's picture of the psyche, initially, no doubt, because of its invocation of sexuality as the focal point of human mental life. To many this was an offensive and unacceptable thesis. Jung, for example, found this orientation too narrow, Freud's account of the personality too naturalistic and reductionistic and proposed, instead, a view of the nature of man which stressed a tension and an emergence from the "transpersonal" content of the unconscious (the *participation mystique,* after Levy-Bruhl) to a state of "individuation" or a variety of self-realization in terms of individualized actualizations of what Jung called the "archetypal motifs."

This general consternation regarding Freudian sexuality (not unlike the reaction accorded to Nietzsche's anti-Christian polemics) retarded in some ways a broader philosophical understanding of the implications of his theory of human nature. It is curious that although Freud died in 1939 (and his important work was published considerably before that time) and an immense amount of attention was paid to his theories in the popular media, it has only been quite recently that any considerable body of philosophical interpretative literature has appeared. This is particularly true regarding the impact of Freudian thought on political philosophy.

Because Freud's ideas stressed sexual sublimation and implicit social permissiveness, were often iconoclastic in tone, and were hostile to the metaphysical claims of religion, it was presumed that they were generally supportive of a radical viewpoint in political and social theory. Many considered Freud's psychology to be an assault upon the very roots of morality. This somewhat premature reaction by those who for other reasons were antagonistic to radicalism was strengthened by Freud's own somewhat offhanded statements of preference for moral relativism and political liberalism and many of the more politically-conscious interpretations of the neo-Freudians (an obvious example is Eric Fromm). Indeed, Herbert Marcuse, now identified with the revolutionary-oriented Left, earlier in his career claimed the inspiration of Freud (as in Marcuse's *Eros and Civilization*).

In the light of more deliberate reflection, it would appear that the contentions of Freud regarding the human personality have a distinctly different ethical and political import. In fact, vitalism in general (Nietzschean, Bergsonian, or Freudian) appears to reinforce the case of those who would argue for the efficacy of trans-societal transmission, the universality of human nature and the indispensability of social control. Freud's indirect contributions to social and political thought are suggestive of a type of neo-classicism in axiological philosophy.

By the beginning of the twentieth century, popular political liberalism had come to rest on a number of philosophical presumptions, among which were relativism, environmentalism and individualism. The relativism of the liberal outlook was both ethical and cultural, buttressed by the growing pre-eminence of a social science strongly dominated by neo-positivistic tenets. Among these tenets was a physicalistic reductionism that, in psychological terms, sought to trace the origins of human behavior to the physiological. It is not accidental that a philosopher like John Dewey, an excellent example of twentieth century liberalism, proceeded from the behavioristic psychology of John Watson. Historically, the crux of relativism was a claim for the uniqueness and irreducibility of subjective experience predicated upon the sovereignty of consciousness. The absence of a basis for universal moral judgment in relativism sprang not only from its positivistic anti-metaphysical bias, but also from its bifurcation of physical process and consciousness. If consciousness was generated in some elemental fashion from the physical faculties, it then became operatively autonomous and directive, particularly as it applied to choice and judgment, even if it was considered to be no more than a "problem-solving" mechanism. The "self-interest" ethnic (from Hume on) assumed that the fundamental human decisions were conducted in the realm of consciousness. Freud, on the other hand, not only denied that this was true, but also posited that the vital ingredient in human behavior, including choice and judgment, represented a universal structure, a priori to experience and partly deterministic in effect. Freud had revived the idea of universal innate ideas, framed in a vitalistic ontology.

Indeed, the word "ideas" is fair to employ, since, certainly, categories such as id, ego, and super-ego, plus a variety of other Freudian categories, are hardly empirically verifiable cognates, their existence being sustained by an argument to logical necessity. The primacy of the psychic (illustrated, perhaps, at its fullest in Freud's "death-wish" theory in *Beyond the Pleasure Principle*) over the material struck directly at the foundational aspect of relativism. While definitions of norms in Freud are situational in cultural terms, that is that standards of behavior reflect evolving conventions, they arise from a universal psyche involved in dealing with cultural phenomena. Thus, concepts of "health" cannot be totally internalized—a culture and its moral norms can be judged beyond some appeal to internal utility.

Freud hits equally at environmentalism. The doctrine of social salvation by environmental engineering flies in the face of Freud's estimation of the inescapable psychological determinants, among which are the persistence of latent aggressiveness. Not denying the desirability of creating conditions conducive to an optimum emotional adjustment, Freud simply rejects the ability of external structure to ameliorate the psychic conflicts.

Taken from another direction, Freud's views are a remarkably vitalistic historicism. The psychic content is an accumulation; "memories" of the past, involved with subrational transmissions that shape human responses to the external world. Civilization is a set of arrangements, practices, and attitudes that patinate an ancient knowledge, a sensitivity to the primordial past, a recurring reminder of an era in which the demands of the libido were given more amplified and uncomplicated expression. Social membership in a civilized society involved, for Freud, the abandonment of the direct exercise of sexual and hostile drives, but they are never totally either forgotten or renounced, merely compensated for by society's preference of acceptable substitutions.

At first glance, Freud's thought would appear to be a vigorous individualism, but the thrust of his ego psychology may be misjudged in this connection. Freud increasingly came to accept the social bond as critical because in its repression of libidinal aims it redirected psychic energies away from egocentricity—self-love—toward a sense of higher loyalty, toward affection, toward the voluntary acceptance of obedience based upon that affection. Freud laid great stress upon the imperative of social identification as crucial to the healthy ego, to the conscience-like operation of the super-ego. This identification, this social cohesion, is dependent upon the emergence of authority—and he views the family as more than merely an Oedipal drama; in this unit is seen the seminal emergence of social authority. Leadership is sufficiently vital to the social process so that there emerges in Freud (far more so in Jung) a variety of elitism which in Freud appears as an attempt to socialize the father-son relationship, investing leadership with a certain psychological legitimacy.

The clear question posed by Freudian psychology is the issue of social control because, by implication, the human psyche presents distinct challenges to the maintenance of social harmony and order. The primary means of such control, Freud contends, is the social approximation of latent satisfactions by the reproduction of political relationships embracing fundamental emotional needs; he cites armies and the Catholic Church as examples of the successful use of surrogates. But beyond these principally psychological observations, the impetus in Freud is directed toward the means by which society, compensatorily if necessary, restrains the natural inclinations. Although Freud's purpose was not to provide answers to this question in terms of the rigor demanded by the political specialist, his psychology puts the question more acutely than anyone since Burke. Similar to the classical moralists, Freud's theory is eventually a restatement of an ancient query: how can society be constructed so as to permit the fullest extent of self-realization, while simultaneously preserving society and, by implication, the individual himself from the ravages of the primitive impulses? Freud's general answer, it can be concluded, is not unlike that of Plato: it is best accomplished by the molding of the human awareness by the efficacious activities of an ethically enlightened political order. It can be presumed that this influence upon behavior, didactic and exemplary, can hold the use of overt coercion to a minimum, but the question of what course to take if these societal restraints fail have concerned virtually every major political thinker from Plato to the present. Freud represents a figure of tremendous dimension in what might be termed a neo-Augustinian reaction against the facile meliorism of the last century. Although he did retain an enduring commitment to the idea of social progress, it was a view tempered by the actualities uncovered in his bold explorations of the hidden and often frightening depths of the human psyche.

RECONCILIATION WITH THE NATURAL IMPERATIVE

Sigmund Freud, like many another European intellectual, was distraught by the savagery of the First World War, a then unparalleled conflict since the horrors of the Thirty Years War. His later writings announce this sense of urgency concerning the possibility of man's retrogression into a state of barbaric hostility. His correspondence with such fellow-intellectuals as Thomas Mann and Stefan Zweig indicate this, as well as displaying a lively appreciation of the ominous events that were taking place in Germany. The "abyss" referred to by Nietzsche was uncovered before the eyes of men to see. Yet Freud was spared, in a manner of speaking, the fresher terrors that began in 1939. The calamitous effect of that world-wide conflict was to leave its peculiar impress upon the philosophical mind. Much of that response would have troubled both Nietzsche and Freud.

Nietzsche, for his part, would have been aroused by the mood of nihilism that arose in the war's wake, a tone of existential hopelessness, a mounting reliance on political shamanism and mass manipulation, a crassness of taste, and a dulling of the creative imagination. He would have denounced the widening prerogatives of the state, whether dictatorial or welfare-centered, and the accelerated decay of individual self-sufficiency.

Freud would have been markedly alarmed by the deepening pathological quality of social life and, indeed, efforts to construct bizarre social utopias resting upon those very same pathological ingredients. He would have been distressed that his theories of psychological hedonism would be twisted into a justification for licentious self-indulgence and a politicalization of social interplay that would offend his primary definitions of its character. He would have been especially disquieted by the increase in the levels and range of violence, indicative of a rising failure of control, both psychological and social in nature—such violence often stemming from a ruthless extirpation of man's instinctual needs. He might wonder, too, if the limits of aberrational life-patterns would be reached in this century, thus creating a mass psychosis that would sweep away civilization as surely as if the Mongol hordes had devastated the known world.

The critical significance of the contributions of Nietzsche and Freud for political philosophy is that they provide an enriched understanding of human pathology, individual and collective, that force one back from hubristic complacencies to the perennial humanistic concerns that have dominated the history of social thought.

Moreover, they invite a necessary reconciliation with nature long neglected in modern philosophy, a restoration of relationship not on the terms of human artifice, but on the terms of the natural imperative.

THE REDIRECTION OF ANTHROPOLOGICAL OUTLOOKS

Carl Gustav Jung not only departs from Freudian orthodoxy, but, in some ways, returns to a more explicitly Nietzschean orientation. In any case, he propounds a philosophy of personality far more dependent than Freud's upon philosophical conjecture. It may be for this reason that Jung's *analytical psychology* has stimulated a lively movement in contemporary anthropology.

Although it is true that Jung's initial break with Freud resulted from Jung's dissatisfaction with the Freudian sexual emphasis, ultimately, Jung presents a view of the human personality significantly different from that of his erstwhile psychoanalytic associate. Jung's conception of "individuation," the emergence of psychic autonomy from the domination of the "transpersonal," the *participation mystique,* is suggestive of a social hierarchy. This is a predominantly aristocratic view and was developed by Erich Neumann, a Jung disciple, in his "Great Men" theory.

Jung's psychology (which is really more a philosophical *Weltanschauung*) revives Nietzsche's distinction between the "herd men" and the men of extraordinary psychological development, tantamount to genius, albeit in less abrasive terms. If doubts can be raised regarding the ultimate compatibility of Freud's view of the human being and the traditional tenets of democracy, then Jung's suppositions form a basis for a new and comprehensive hierarchicalism. As Jung once observed, "Nature is aristocratic."

Even neo-Freudian modifications do not explicitly blunt the substantive attack of depth psychology on the precepts of nineteenth century individualism. What is shared between the "motive-torque" or "depth" psychological theorists and individualism is the concept of universal egocentricity, the imperative of ego gratification as a basis for human behavior. But there the similarity ceases.

The Freudian or vitalistic viewpoint assumes that this universal egocentricity arises itself from *universals,* inherent and innate configurations of the psyche, as against a "self-interest" doctrine that presupposes wholly nominalistic or subjective responses to particular environmental situations. This distinction may be best put in terms of the range of options open to individual choice, judgment, and action. The Freudian conception drastically limits these options in contrast to the greater possibilities presented by "self-interest" individualism. This limitation of individual options is reflected in a limitation of social options, at least to the extent that a normative conception of a "healthy" or "sick" society emerges. The Freudians are thus ranged against the followers of Bentham.

A normative view of society thus stimulated by Freudian and post-Freudian psychological theory provokes a new and redirected anthropology. It does so in two ways: (1) it implicitly denies historical theories of social atomism (still preserved in large part by major anthropological schools); (2) it seeks, by various means, including mythological and historical analysis, an explanation for the organic nature of society and its normative character and, in so doing, argues against cultural relativism.

This new anthropological orientation is buttressed by other influences than those identifiable with Freud and his followers, although some of these influences have strong vitalistic overtones. Vitalism became a more highly refined philosophical stance in the hands of persons like Henri Bergson, particularly, with his doctrine of the *élan vital.* It, in part, affected the development of panpsychism, as expounded by the so-called "process philosophers," A. N. Whitehead, Alexander, and Hartmann. Biological investigations, particularly among the "ethologists," Tinbergen and Lorenz, reinforce not only the metaphysical universality of vitalism and panpsychism, but revive and amplify the role of instinct in human behavior and suggest a deeper integration of human behavior and social structure with non-hominid nature.

To the social philosopher, these tendencies are provocative as they contribute to emerging anthropological concepts in which social evolution and "super-organic" factors loom larger. Such anthropological speculation at once challenges the idealistic metaphysic as it does the reductionistic theories of human nature inherited from the nineteenth century. As Nicolai Hartmann wrote in his *New Ways of Ontology*:

> The new anthropology rediscovers these relationships' spiritual and non-spiritual factors. It has room for the autonomy of spiritual life but knows, also, how to unite with it at the organic stratum of the human being. That is possible only on the basis of certain ontological ideas. The absolute self-sufficiency of the spirit as defended by idealist theories cannot be maintained. But the autonomy of the spirit does not depend on doctrines of this type which are at variance with the phenomena. All the independence of the spirit which we know is independence in dependence, and the dependence is a weighty and many-sided one. To dispute this dependence would be closing one's eyes to the facts. But a reconciliation of dependence with independence can be accomplished only by an ontological clarification of the basic relationship between the heterogeneous strata of reality. (pp. 41–42)

The "bridge" of vitalism, from the nineteenth century to the twentieth, is highly significant in terms of *ontology* and *personality* —both of which have contributed to the evolution of social and political thought. The ontological perspective of the vitalists and process philosophers, from Nietzsche to the present, has contributed to a new naturalistic emphasis in social thought in which the problem of the natural hierarchy is reintroduced and nature reappraised as a model for human conduct and social organization. The ontological preoccupations of post-Nietzschean vitalism have essentially preserved a metaphysical connection between speculative and axiological philosophy, expressed in social terms in the doctrines of *hierarchy* and *inheritance* as pertinent to social theory.

Even more dramatic was vitalism's impact on the philosophy of human nature on both the philosophical and ideological levels. It raised grave doubt as to the sufficiency, if not the entire viability, of cognitive human reason, and it dealt a severe blow to the primacy of consciousness. It, also, indirectly brought into question many of the empirically-grounded assumptions that served as a foundation for political liberalism and its predilection for human educability, as well as its assertion of the validity of free, subjective judgment.

But perhaps the most profound effect of vitalism was to vividly remind humankind of its animal heritage and connections, its ontological and psychological dependence upon "brute nature." This influence swung the pendulum away from the facile optimisms of the nineteenth century and restored a recognition of an almost forgotten side of human nature: the presence of the primordial self: dark, hidden, violent, rapacious. The First World War seemed to reinforce the gloomy Nietzschean prediction regarding the course of the culture. Also Freud's shocking revelations of the innate character of the human unconscious seemed to take social and political form, as the established order of western society showed signs of crumbling in the early decades of the century, and the spectre of totalitarian repression appeared.

At the same time, a reverberating motif of vitalism was health, either Nietzsche's liberation of the "sovereign individual" or Freud's therapeutic discoveries or Jung's quest for the fulfillment of the soul. If the vitalistic tradition exhibited a certain pessimism regarding some of the flattering estimations of human nature contained in idealism and classical liberalism, it also pointed to social measures through which a new era of psychological well-being might be achieved. This would be accomplished largely by reordering priorities regarding social control and permissiveness, in varying relationships in diverse areas of social life. It injected into the twentieth century a tone of radical experimentation that disturbed established political and social categories and helped to lay a base for the sharply innovative political tendencies of the post-World War I era.

At base, vitalism offered a new concept of ethical accountability in which the norms of individual and social behavior were to be found engrained in the natural fabric of existence. It participated intensely in the rapid secularization of the culture that increasingly has characterized the century, not by denying spirituality (which even Nietzsche does not do), but by replacing a supernatural account of it with what Hartmann called a "spiritualistic naturalism," a monistic ontological view that made of spirit the common property of all existence and morality not merely the ordinances revealed by an allegedly unique human reason.

In many ways, vitalism, even of the Freudian variety, reasserts the objective and universal status of value, as against versions of moral relativism. But it does so by a radical inversion of the ontological hierarchy: value actualization proceeds *upward* from the lowest strata of existence rather than value viewed as an imposition from a supernatural or transcendental source. The effects of such a viewpoint militate against any articulated, verbalized canon or catalogue of moral strictures and obligations, but, rather, stress subrational responses to value, actualized in subjective encounter.

Where does this leave a "civic ethic," upon which, presumably, a stable political order could rest? Nietzsche asserts that his outlook desirably abolishes such an ethic, such an ethic being only the conspiratorial machination of the inherently inferior. But that viewpoint is not shared by the later vitalists who tend to look at the social order in more organic terms. If society or community is not an "idea" in the neo-Hegelian sense nor is it an artifice of self-conscious individuals, it may well be a natural form responding to its own ethical mandates and, further, the interpretation of those social ethical directives may fall upon those who enjoy a particular affinity with the "ground norms" of the society. The sum effect of late vitalism was to reemphasize an organic societal structure and a hierarchical or even aristocratic social ethic; it sought to redefine the relationship of the individual and the social order, not in terms of "man versus the state" or in terms of the total absorption of the individual into an objectified, autonomous social "destiny," but to understand, if possible, the psychic ties which bind men together and also to social responsibility.

FOR ADDITIONAL READING

BERGSON, HENRI, *The Creative Mind* (trans. by Mabelle Andison). New York: Philosophical Library, 1945.

ELIADE, MIRCEA, *Cosmos and History: the Myth of the Eternal Return* (trans. by W. R. Trask). New York: Harper, 1959 (orig. pub. 1949).

FINGARETTE, HERBERT, *The Self in Transformation: Psychoanalysis, Philosophy and the Life of the Spirit.* New York: Basic Books, 1963.

FREUD, SIGMUND, *General Introduction to Psychoanalysis* (trans. by Joan Riviere). Garden City, New York: Doubleday, 1943 (orig. pub. 1920).

GOLDBRUNNER, JOSEF, *Individuation: A Study of the Depth Psychology of Carl Gustav Jung* (trans. by Stanley Godman). New York: Pantheon, 1956.

HARTMANN, NICOLAI, *New Ways of Ontology* (trans. by R. C. Kuhn). Chicago: Henry Regnery, 1953.

JUNG, C. G., *Modern Man in Search of His Soul* (trans. by W. S. Dell and C. F. Baynes). New York: Harcourt, Brace, 1933.

KAUFMANN, WALTER, *Nietzsche: Philosopher, Psychologist, Anti-Christ.* New York: Meridian Books (World Publishing Co.), 1956 (orig. pub. 1950).

NEUMANN, ERICH, *The Origins and History of Consciousness* (trans. by R. F. C. Hull). New York: Bollingen Foundation, 1954 (orig. pub. 1949).

NIETZSCHE, FRIEDRICH, *The Philosophy of Nietzsche.* New York: Modern Library, 1927.

PROGOFF, IRA, *Jung's Psychology and Its Social Meaning.* New York: Grove Press, 1955.

RICOEUR, PAUL, *Freud and Philosophy* (trans. by Denis Savage). New Haven: Yale University Press, 1970.

ROAZEN, PAUL, *Freud: Political and Social Thought.* New York: Knopf, 1968.

THREE

The Return of the Primal Horde

Fascism

On the general assumption that *fascism* as a social doctrine is distasteful to those espousing the traditional Judeo-Christian values, a wide variety of people are "blamed," for its creation. The list is rather baffling, to include Plato, Machiavelli, Hobbes, Vico, Fichte, Rousseau, Hegel, Gobineau, Nietzsche, Sorel, and Pareto, to name but a few.

No socio-political theory of the magnitude of fascism can appear without substantial antecedents, but it may be well to recall that the explicit term *fascism* originally had a quite restricted meaning. The term is Italian (taken from *fasces*, the bundle of sticks appearing in the standard of the Roman legions) and refers to a specific version of state syndicalism developed by Benito Mussolini. The term, of course, soon came to have a wider application, although the crux of its definition still involved the economic organization of the society, to wit, a state built upon the existence of private monopolies, under governmental concession, supported by a controlled and regimented work force.

Fascism, thus, must be looked at in two ways: its more limited development as an off-shoot of syndicalism and its broader context, involving a wider range of historical and philosophical influences, culminating in the totalitarian society, exemplified in its extreme form in Germany under the National Socialists (1932–1945).

It may be appropriate to examine fascism in its more restricted sense first. It is possible to deal with the emergence of fascism in both ideological and sociological terms. To trace the ideological development from earlier theories of syndicalism, particularly those of Sorel, is one thing, but to explain its political emergence and, in certain countries, its temporary success is yet another. It should be remembered that as a social phenomenon, fascism, of various national varieties, emerges as a response to deep social crisis and in its European expression was largely triggered by a feeling of desperate frustration and insecurity on the part of the middle classes—to some extent, fascism is a revolt of the petit bourgeoisie.

The ruinous effects of World War I had projected three major political ideologies into a contest for the control of the states of Europe, their relative strengths dependent in large measure upon the degree of social and economic dislocation. These ideologies included: (1) a loose coalition of elements of liberalism, including the non-Marxist "social democratic" movements; (2) Marxism, incorporated, by and large, in the international communist movement; (3) varieties of fascism. In relatively stable countries, such as Great Britain, the preponderance of political influence still lay with the liberal coalition, although even here, as in the general strike of 1926, Marxist and fascist elements were clearly visible. Besides militant socialists, a British fascist movement began in 1923 and three years later was reported to have enlisted one half million members. In 1933, the British Union of Fascists, under Sir Oswald Mosley, a former Labour Party cabinet minister, was formed and became a not inconsiderable political factor. Although Mosley's British fascists were, essentially, an off-shoot from the extreme Left, other right-wing factions expressed some sympathy for fascist-type policies.

In France, exhausted by the rigors of the war, the hold of the liberals was less secure. Communist and fascist movements were more formidable. Charles Maurras and his *Action Francaise,* in some aspects akin to the fascist outlook, was a force to be reckoned with.

The deterioration of national stability and morale were acute in Italy, the position of the moderates more precarious, due in part to a serious fragmentization of the liberal coalition. Socialism was on the move; the choice was between a Marxist-style alternative or the National Syndicalism of Mussolini and his *Squadristi.* There appeared in Italy an element only partially perceivable in Franco-British radical phalanxes: the willingness on the part of both communist and fascist contenders to employ violence and terror to gain political control. The age of the coup d'état had arrived. Private armies, retained by various political action groups, became more potent than the nominal security forces of the state.

Germany had become a social and economic wasteland fought over by bands of political adventurers taking advantage of the paralysis of the liberal-constituted "Weimar Republic": communists, the "Storm Battalions" of the National Socialists, and the so-called "Free Corps" made up of uprooted veterans of the late war. The Weimar Republic had lost all authority, physical or moral, and was held together by the paternalistic figure of Field Marshal von Hindenburg. Whipping up the anger and fear of the populace with tales of the Bolshevik threat and the conspiratorial machinations of the Jews, Adolph Hitler, leader of the National Socialists or Nazis, forced himself upon a vulnerable and atrophied government as Chancellor.

The emergence of these fascist movements or parties in major European states revealed certain characteristics in common, but also showed a high degree of national variation. Fascism was—and is —distinctly variable in terms of national settings. Contrast, for example, Nazi fascism with that of Mussolini, the Japanese version (from the "Meiji Restoration" to the MacArthur "shogunate"), Franco's *Falange* in Spain and Peron's movement in Argentina. Consider, even, Huey Long's "reign" in our own state of Louisiana.

In its earliest inception, fascism was a derivation of syndicalism, itself a variation of the idea of the "closed corporate state." A provocative and radical picture of syndicalism is provided by Georges Sorel early in the century.

Sorel had early been influenced by the writings of Marx, but only on a superficial level. Filled with reformist zeal, he had reacted strongly to *l'affaire Dreyfus* and published a collection of essays on syndicalism, beginning in 1898. Syndicalism, in Sorel's hand, was projected as a revolutionary doctrine, inspired, in the broad sense, by Marxism, featuring the political and social pre-eminence of the working class. While accepting the Marxist concept of the class war, syndicalists, like Sorel, rejected the concept of the "dictatorship of the proletariat" and advocated a national system built upon a federation of trade unions and associations of workers (the "syndicals" or "guilds").

Sorel's importance rested with his exposition of the revolutionary aspects of the militant advocacy of syndicalism. In his best-known work, *Reflections on Violence* (1908), Sorel provides a picture of the tactics of social upheaval in which political movements are cast in the roles of "armies"; social warfare is declared to be unavoidable. Quasi-rationalistic theories embraced by Marx are discarded in favor of the spontaneous release of passion and action.

From a purely historical point of view, Sorel is a figure of contradictions; consistency is not an especial merit of the man. He expressed admiration for such otherwise diverse figures as Lenin, Croce, Bergson, and William James. His influence on subsequent communist and fascist thought is debated, but there is a very evident connection between syndicalism and the early forms of fascism and, in Sorel's case, his writings did clearly affect the methodology of fascist political action. While the egalitarian elements in Sorel's viewpoint were rejected by the fascists, his emphasis on the usefulness of violence was retained.

Fascism turned enthusiastically to elitism, particularly as conceived by a school of European sociologists spearheaded by Vilfredo Pareto, Gaetano Mosca and Robert Michels. Pareto, while himself a political liberal, had presented an elaborate theory of social organization that featured an explanation for social leadership based upon what he termed the "circulation of elites," an implicit denial of the primary assumptions of popular government. Mosca argued for the inevitability of a ruling class. Michels, a Swiss sociologist admired by Mussolini, advocated a theory upholding the inevitability of elite rule as an organic feature of social organization, describing what he called the "iron law of oligarchy."

The culmination of the system of the national syndicals thereby became a special, if reasonably broadly based, elite, which became, in turn, the Fascist Party. One-party rule was justifiable, in fascist theory, on two possible grounds: (1) the Party became the consolidated expression of the national will as it embraced, at the apex of the state, the varieties of the subordinate "corporate" wills; (2) the Party became the unique manifestation of the national "soul," the custodian of state destiny. Italian fascism stressed the former, German fascism the latter.

NATIONALISM, IRRATIONALISM, AND MYSTICISM

Fascism was the outgrowth of more than mere syndicalism and elitist sociology. It was also the apotheosis of nationalism, irrationalism, and a rather particular blend of mysticism. Italian fascism, for example, represented a revival of hyper-nationalism—the *risorgimento*—coupled with a somewhat tortured modification of Hegelianism, the latter supplied, in the main, by Giovanni Gentile, an Italian idealist who placed his philosophical services at the disposal of the Fascist Party.

Nationalism (as contrasted to national sentiment) was a phenomenon largely unleashed by the French Revolution. The concept of a unique national superiority began to emerge in the early nineteenth century—one gets a fair look at it in Fichte's *Addresses to the German Nation* early in the nineteenth century. To some extent, this nationalistic fervor can be connected with Romanticism; the idea of a mystic, almost transcendental vision of the Nation can be noted in such literary figures as Wordsworth, Byron, and Schiller. Philosophically, nationalistic feeling was propelled and enhanced by idealism, particularly Hegelianism (especially the early Hegel) and the "organic" or "metaphysical" theory of the state. Moreover, it was stimulated by the flow of political events, the urges for national unification that brought into prominence such figures as Bismarck, Cavour, and Mazzini. The more excessive declarations of nationalism had a distinct tenor of ethnic superiority and historical determinism, as can be witnessed from Herder to von Treitschke to Hitler. Such nationalistic passion was not necessarily racial (e.g., Italian fascism), but it was so in the case of the German and Japanese versions.

Racial theory did form, in many instances, a significant ingredient of fascism. Some of this racial theory purported to be "scientific," tracing its origins to the anthropological speculations of Count Gobineau who contributed the theory of Aryan superiority. The German fascists were especially fascinated with race. Gobineau's superior Aryans quickly became identified as Germans, no doubt prompted by the writings of Houston Stewart Chamberlain. Nordic or Germanic biological superiority became a central tenet of the Nazi dogma, relegating less fit "races" to a position of servitude. The Japanese—as descendants of the Sun God—enjoyed, in their eyes, a comparable pre-eminence, particularly in relationship to the original Caucasoid inhabitants of the Japanese islands.

This hyper-nationalism, often reinforced by acute ethnocentrism, led to the irredentist inclinations of fascist states, the recovery of previously lost territories inhabited by their racial brethren.

The adoration of the Nation, in fascist thought, was supported by a neo-Hegelian theory of the state joined to what has been termed the "myth of the Folk." The first viewpoint, best elucidated by Gentile, is not precisely a neo-Hegelian position in fact, since Gentile substitutes a basically irrationalist theory of the unity of the individual and the state with its subsequent obligations, and he also eliminates a distinction between *thought* and *action,* a favorite tenet of fascist theorists.

The difference between Hegel's and Gentile's theory of the state turns on Hegel's description of the state as a logical Idea emanating from the actualizations of Objective Spirit. The state, for Gentile, is an autonomous entity, enjoying its own destiny, its higher purpose, its more elevated ethical mandate—the state is not an Idea, but a form of ultimate Will, embracing within it all individual wills, thus the will of the state is an extension of the will of the individual. The state is infallible not because it is a projection of the Absolute, but because it is a *total* will, incorporating all human thought and desire. The theory of *totalitarianism* arises from this premise: all that is constituted by human activity legitimately falls within the purview and authority of the state.

Fascism is candidly anti-intellectual—as Gentile points out—because it renounces thought and reflection divorced from action and, of course, because its philosophical base is irrationalistic. The higher call of state duty requires not independent, reflective thought, but total commitment in terms of action. It is even suggested, by Gentile and others, that detached thought is effete and decadent. The moral realization of the individual does not lie in introspection or intellectual assent, but in active participation in the purposes and projects of the state.

It may seem curious, but Gentile claims that fascism is the only political theory that gives adequate expression to human spirituality. In part, this contention develops from the Hegelian view that the moral self-realization of the person can be attained only by the performance of duty to the state as a higher actualization of the Absolute. The fascist concept of "spirituality," however, differs substantially from the Hegelian by assuming that the connections of individual-to-state are not logically-based, but are irrational and transcendental. It also denies the Hegelian concept of *Right* as the objectification of reality delimiting reciprocal relationships between the individual and the state. The fascist version of "spirit" is not Hegelian, but virtually animistic, a pagan recapitulation, in which the human being is seen as a psychic entity requiring, for its maintenance, participation in a higher and more complete psychic authority.

This primitive concept of "spirituality" can be illustrated by the "myth of the Folk" as a formative element in Nation-worship. While there are overtones of this mystic notion in Rousseau, Herder, and Hegel, it becomes surprisingly literal in the postulations of fascist thought. The "people" or "Folk" are seen as an organic continuity tracing its genesis to a primordial state of heroic barbarism. The nature of this continuity and, as well, the organic composition of the "people" is disclosed as a subrational, spiritualistic destiny to which the ongoing generations are bound to contribute and perpetuate. This "Folk Spirit" is a superinforming agency; it directs and shapes the national existence, but knowledge of it—if that is the appropriate word—is not equally distributed. There are exceptional individuals who, to varying degrees, are instruments of this Folk Spirit and privy to its directives by virtue of non-rational "feelings" or intimations. There are, in fact, "prophets" of the national will, in other words, or, as Erich Neumann phrased it, "hypnotized hypnotists."

This variation of *charisma*, this pseudo-religiosity, that invests the personages of the fascist elite explains, in part, the fascist conception of leadership—the *Fuhrerprinzip* in German terminology. The fascist leader is elevated from the anonymity of the Folk by being a carrier of projections emanating from the national spirit. He becomes infallible in judgment as he shares in the self-defining infallibility of the national origins and purposes.

While this motif is characteristic of fascist theory, it varies considerably in intensity and significance in each national manifestation. Certain fascist regimes have featured a plural headship, as in Japan (although the figure of the emperor became a focal point of national reverence). Moreover, the articulation of the fascist leader as the infallible prophet is restricted, by and large, to the rank and file and not to his immediate subordinates. Indeed, a considerable degree of instability can be noted in the higher echelons of fascist regimes, revealing power struggles of an intense and often uninhibited sort. The means by which fascist leadership gains power and clothes itself with a putative legitimacy tend to introduce techniques of power acquisition that emphasize conspiracy and violence. It is an interesting question whether fascist dogma, especially of the more extreme mystical types, is the sincere commitment of the leadership or merely a device or rationale for the usurpation of political power. The answer to this question is confused by the fact that fascist leaders themselves have been of distinctly variable personalities, some giving evidence of severe emotional aberration (as with Hitler) as against others who appear altogether rational in the clinical sense, such as Franco or Peron. The hypothesis has been advanced that fascism is best explained in general terms by analyzing it as a psychological pathology. The case has been well-argued by Eric Fromm, among others. Such a viewpoint, however, seems overly preoccupied with the Nazi phenomenon and does not offer an adequate explanation for other forms of fascism. Although the philosophic base of fascism is undeniably and overtly irrationalistic, this is not a *prima facie* argument that fascism can be explained as a form of social madness. Fascist theories of leadership do not rest exclusively on a mystic vision of the omnicompetent leader, a *Fuhrer* (literally, "leader") or a *Duce* (literally, "guide" or "captain"). Fascism endorses, too, a more classical concept of the virtues of autocracy. Fascist emphasis upon the maximization of unity and the downward flow of authority through the rigid political and social hierarchy implies the necessity for locating ultimate power in a single will or in a tiny cabal of the super-elite. This is thought of by fascists as enhancing efficiency, since its over-arching preoccupation is with action as against deliberation. The concept provides a concentration of national energies and resources, in preference to the "muddling through" proclivities of pluralistic democracies with their equilibriumistic foundations. This drastic simplification of the allocation of power is viewed an efficacious means of responding to social crisis and avoiding the jeopardies of societal decadence.

The concept that fascism is a necessary response to social decadence is revealed in its preoccupation with *strength* as a cardinal virtue. Fascism is, in part, a neo-barbarism, exalting in the primal strengths and simplicities; it accepts, in other words, half of the Nietzschean dictum: it is solely Dionysian and lauds the warrior instincts at the cost of the creative and artistic. It relishes the use of force, not merely as a handy instrument, but for itself, the awesome expression of the "memory of the primal horde." It invariably introduces a warrior society, a "barracks state," not exclusively for the purposes of social control, but also because its implicit value orientations are warlike and imperial. Its ultimate social model is the Folk-Horde with technological embellishments.

This neo-barbaric predisposition of fascism expresses itself in an emphasis on the potency of symbolism and its manipulation. Indeed, fascism embraces a bewildering variety of techniques to reinforce the mass identifications it requires, reminiscent of the calculated devices described in Plato's *Laws* to maximize social cohesion. It posits a "closed environment" in which human existence is carefully structured so as to enhance the amenability of the individual to the state and to destroy any consciousness of individual autonomy.

THE USES OF TERROR

Although many of its methods in this regard are psychologically exhortatory and invested with a certain spiritualistic persuasion, fascist theory accepts the inevitability of coercion, but conceives it as being an instrumentality far beyond customary concepts of legal restraint. A fascist state may well be a "constitutional" state if, by that, one means a political entity featuring a constitutional instrument. That "constitution," however, has no binding force upon the national will as articulated by the leadership; it is merely a series of commands, a proclamation of positive law. Most fascist states, although not all, have produced rather elaborate legal codes, but they do not define or confine governmental authority or power, but express the obligations due from the body politic. Law, in fascist thought, is much like the view of it held by Rousseau; it is a proclamation of the "general will."

Thus the coercive power of the state is not constrained by laws or constitutions; it is candidly despotic, if allegedly benevolent. The coercive power of the state is justified not on the basis of insuring individual "right" or the security of the general welfare, but upon the prerogative enjoyed by the state in pursuit of its own goals and purposes. There is, in consequence, no theoretical limits to the coercive power of the state. This allegation, coupled with fascism's neo-primitive view of human nature and its fascination with strength, lead to what has been appropriately termed the "institutionalization of terror."

The uses of terror as a political device have an ancient history. In the main, terror has been employed for purposes of intimidation in two circumstances: (1) as a means of securing existing instrumentalities of power; (2) to serve as a "corrective" means by rulers, usually directed against irreconcilables and dissidents. The French Revolution provides the classic exposition of the political use of terror both in its revolutionary application and as a counteractive force against those in opposition to the new regime.

The contribution of fascism was to conceive of the uses of terror beyond their revolutionary or corrective functions by "institutionalizing" it as an on-going feature of governmental behavior. While principally coercive in its intent, fascist terror also provided a type of social catharsis in which popular frustrations and inclinations for vengeance could be symbolically sublimated by acts of terror and persecution against alleged "enemies of the state." No political regime can continue indefinitely solely on the basis of its ability to introduce terror; a certain assent is required and fascist regimes have acquired that assent in some instances, suggestive of the fact that terror, considering its limitations, has a diversified purpose.

Terror as a consistent aspect of governmental activity is usually developed if the regime in power is insufficiently stable to dispense with it or if the aims of the regime are so all-encompassing that terror is a necessary instrument in the attainment of these social ends. The latter use is more characteristic of fascist practice. If the degree of repression sought requires the implementation of terror, the options open to those against whom the terror is potentially directed are substantially closed, save for the employment of counter-terror. Thus, fascism assumes a perpetual state of terror and counter-terror, requiring the maintenance of specific agencies concerned with its employment.

The presence of terror and the agencies directing its use vary sharply in specific fascist experiences and even theoretical pronouncements. More secure fascist states appear to almost dispense with it altogether, but they never completely abandon its use, especially against internal opponents equally devoted to its employment.

Any potential punitive act has a certain intimidating character, sufficient, indeed, to restrain certain types of presumably antisocial conduct. Terror, in contrast, is the threat or execution of physical or mental torment so severe and appalling that it may have the desired effect of virtually incapacitating the will to resist.

Fascism, among other contemporary political creeds, has sought to legitimize terror as a social technique. This legitimization of terror turns upon a simple hypothesis repeatedly emphasized in fascist theory: the "end," indeed, "justifies the means."

Terror, itself morally suspect, is held to be ethically acceptable as it is presumably employed for commendable moral ends.

Ranged against this viewpoint is the Kantian insistence that persons must always be considered as "ends" and never as "means." Kant takes sides on a very old ethical controversy: is the moral criterion to be established on the basis of the intrinsic nature of the act or choice or, conversely, upon its consequences? Is lying inherently wrong or should failing to tell the truth be judged by its specific moral consequences? The latter point of view is sometimes called *voluntarism*—and fascism, along with other essentially radical political ideologies, takes an extreme voluntaristic position. Fascist theory renders it difficult to talk reasonably about criminality (apart from violations of the positive law of the state). It tends to reduce moral discussion to irrationalist intuitions of a "higher" will, represented, phenomenally, by the totalitarian state.

FASCISM: A FORM OF POLITICAL RADICALISM

This extreme view of morality is but one of a number of reasons why fascism is correctly catalogued as a form of political radicalism. It is often supposed that fascism represents the most extreme end of the ideological continuum designated as the Right. In like fashion, communism, another variety of radicalism, is placed on the extreme Left. These terminologies—Right and Left—are philosophically confusing. Regardless of the immense differences that exist between fascism and communism, both are forms of radicalism. Both are drastic departures from traditional or customary social beliefs and practices, involving a foundational reconstruction of existing social forms. To the journalist, the political Right is suggestive of those social theories in varying degrees hostile to the tenets of popular democracy, especially its seminal commitment to social equality. "Radicalism" he consigns to the Left as being increasingly "collectivistic" or "egalitarian."

This is an awkward way of establishing ideological classifications. Certainly communism is equally antagonistic to the precepts of popular democracy—regardless of its invocation of the term "democratic"—as is fascism and is equally desirous of radical reconstruction of those social arrangements that do not conform to the communist paradigm. Both range as opponents, from different directions, of the main currents of social evolution. Both are vigorously "statist" in preference and contemptuous of individualism as a social precept.

Fascism does not logically fit, historically, on the political Right, if that term in any way is connected with conservative or aristocratic ideas. In most actual instances, fascist movements have been most strenuously opposed by "conservatives," as communism has had as its principal foe, the "social democrats." The opposition to Hitler largely came from old-line German conservatives and social democrats down to and including the "bomb plot" of 1944. In Italy, the conservatives and monarchists opposed the *Fascisti;* Benedetto Croce (identified, philosophically, with the Right) went under virtual house arrest in the Mussolini period, later to serve in the liberated Italian government after the Allied invasion. Ortega y Gasset, the prominent Rightist Spanish philosopher, went into exile with the fall of the Republican government to General Franco. Even in Japan, the conservative elements, represented in part by ranking officers of the Imperial Navy, sought to control the militaristic and expansionistic policies of the Army clique under Premier Tojo. The *Peronistas* of Argentina were hardly bedfellows of that country's right-wing factions. Consider, too, the present fate of conservatives in Greece. The pattern is observable also in political controversy in countries that did not actually partake of the fascist "experiment."

"Fascism" or "fascist" have become terms much bandied about as ideological pejoratives. To some, they are words loosely applied to any point of view or person thought to be to the political Right of Chairman Mao. This indiscriminate usage has, perhaps, obscured the fact that bona fide fascist theory and its sympathizers are not yet historical curiosities. Fascism, to some, remains an attractive alternative. Apart from arguing whether or not the governments of certain present states are, in fact, fascist in character (e.g., the present government of Greece), fascist movements are still to be observed in several countries: the Carlists in Spain, certain factions in France, neo-fascist groups in Germany and Italy, to say nothing of home-grown varieties in Latin America—plus extremist groups even in Britain and the United States.

Two seemingly contradictory concepts identify fascist movements:

1. Fascism has always taken on a distinctly national flavor and character; it fits the idiom of the country, so to speak. It reflects, in part, the peculiar national configurations.

2. At the same time, fascism does have a fairly specific philosophical base: it endorses a pervasively irrationalistic concept of knowledge; it is activistic and anti-intellectual; it rests upon ethnocentrism, hyper-nationalism, and geographic and historical determinism; it presupposes a "myth of the Folk" and often a theory of racial superiority; it embraces a doctrine of the inevitability of elites, a "metaphysical" concept of the state and a totalitarian view of state power; it admires strength and force as indicators of barbaric rejuvenation; it features a concept of the infallibility of the leader-prophet or its plural equivalent; and, finally, it sponsors employment of terror and repression as legitimate political techniques.

Fascism is interesting to examine if only because it is one of the most extravagant reactions against a rationalistic conception of the means of dealing with social problems. It is produced by a profound discouragement regarding the potency of human reason.

As long as the cultural malaise remains intense and the conditions of life continue to produce intolerable anxieties and savage insecurities, fascism will remain an ideological option. Fascism reflects a fervent yearning for simplicity, the reintroduction of elemental assurances, at the price of restricting the play of the human imagination and social talent.

FOR ADDITIONAL READING

ARENDT, HANNAH, *The Origins of Totalitarianism*. New York: Meridian Books (World Publishing Co.), 1958.

FINER, HERMAN, *Mussolini's Italy*. New York: Grosset & Dunlap, 1965 (orig. pub. 1935).

GENTILE, GIOVANNI, *Genesis and Structure of Society* (trans. by H. S. Harris). Urbana, Ill.: University of Illinois Press, 1963 (orig. pub. 1946).

GREGOR, J. A., *Contemporary Radical Ideologies: Totalitarian Thought in the Twentieth Century*. New York: Random House, 1968.

GRUNBERGER, RICHARD, *The 12-Year Reich: A Social History of Nazi Germany, 1933–1945*. New York: Ballantine Books, 1972.

MICHELS, ROBERT, *Political Parties: A Sociological Study of Oligarchical Tendencies of Modern Democracies* (trans. by E. and C. Paul). New York: Collier Books (Macmillan), 1962.

MUSSOLINI, BENITO, "The Doctrine of Fascism" in *Social and Political Philosophy*, J. Somerville, and R. E. Santon, eds. Garden City, New York: Doubleday, 1963.

NOLTE, ERNEST, *Three Faces of Fascism* (trans. by Leila Vennevitz). New York: Mentor Books (New American Library), 1965.

SCHNEIDER, H. W., *Making the Fascist State*. New York: Oxford University Press, 1928.

STERN, FRITZ, *The Politics of Cultural Despair*. Berkeley: University of California Press, 1961.

VIERECK, PETER, *Metapolitics: The Roots of the Nazi Mind*. New York: Capricorn Books (Putnam's), 1961.

WEBBER, E., *Varieties of Fascism*. Princeton: Van Nostrand Reinhold, 1964.

FOUR

The Materialist Utopia

Communism

In 1906, V. I. Lenin asked in a well-known essay, *What Is to be Done?* It was a double-barreled question, because he not only faced the theoretical problem of promoting a revolutionary reconstitution of the social order, but, as well, he realized the necessity of translating the more-or-less academic reflections of Karl Marx into an effective program of political action. After all, Lenin was not only a theoretician, but also a politician and a practicing revolutionary—who would eventually personally direct the first state to be governed under the principles of communism.

In temperament, Lenin stood in sharp contrast to his intellectual mentor, Marx. Marx was an observer, almost a recluse, possessed of an incisive analytical mind and a man who considered himself to be primarily a scientist. Lenin was given to astute political judgment; he was a tactician, a manager, a pamphleteer, a personality attuned to the requirements of political activity.

LENIN'S REVISIONISM

His problem, once convinced of the rightness of the Marxist world-view, was to forge the philosophy of "dialectical materialism" into a political credo, indeed, a sort of secular religion that would grip the imaginations of men, men unable, in the main, to appreciate the intricacies of *Das Kapital.* The project of recapitulating Marxist doctrine into a popular social creed and a basis for political strategy was not simple, and it could not be accomplished without some quite significant modifications of "pure" Marxist thought.

It is perhaps ironical that Marx, the avowed intellectual, conceived that the leadership of the revolution would be provided exclusively by the proletariat. Such a conclusion was inescapable because only the conditions of life experienced by the working classes could produce the ideological insights required to spearhead the eventual revolution. Lenin, the practical politician, on the other hand, was unwilling to believe that the proletarians, unaided, could provide the crucial leadership demanded and tended, as a result, to place his trust in intellectuals or, more specifically, *declassé* intellectuals who, as an act of intellectual cognizance, made common cause with the proletariat and would thus occupy positions of revolutionary leadership.

This is not an insignificant distinction between Marx and Lenin—and it helps to explain the development of Leninist elitism in both theory and practice. Marx, consistent with his basic philosophical premises, assumed that all ideological conviction arose from economic circumstances, from the translation of rudimentary economic relationships (of the "exploited" and the "exploiters") into cognitive bodies of ideas. He even explains the phenomenon of art in this fashion.

It follows that not only is the proletariat the only truly "revolutionary" class, but that it also produces, internally, its own ideology and leadership. It cannot be forthcoming from any other source, Marx insists, because no other segment of society, within the context of the "class war," enjoys a comparable set of economic circumstances that produce a genuine revolutionary perspective and motivation.

In the history of communist theory, from Lenin to Mao, this was the first "pure" Marxist concept to receive substantial "revision."

Lenin certainly had doubts about this Marxist axiom. One possible source of his skepticism might have been the fact that he proposed starting a revolution in Russia where a proletariat—of the explicit type described by Marx—did not substantially exist. Marx had predicted that the communist revolution was most likely to commence in Germany or Britain, the most advanced industrial states in Europe, and he would have been shocked, no doubt, that it, in fact, took place in industrially-backward Russia. But then Marx did not fully appreciate the intellectual climate of Russia, or perceive the connections between certain drifts in Russian thought—anarchism, Narodnikism, or even the Tolstoyan reification of the thought of the Folk—and the contentions of communism, soon to be Bolshevism. Marx, after all, took his economic reductionist theories seriously, indeed.

But Lenin's misgivings regarding the proletariat's ability to provide its own leadership were prompted by other factors. Lenin had the politician's grasp of the organizational imperative and the requirements of mass manipulation. To him, the revolution would require its "educators"; the idea of the "dictatorship of the proletariat" implied the "rule of the elite." These "educators" would have to be ideologists; an elite would have to be defined as a body of persons possessing an especially complete knowledge of the dogmatic ideology and its ramifications. This meant, to Lenin, the recruitment of intellectuals and their subsequent extraordinary training in the casuistic applications of ideology.

But the elite could not, in the same breath, consist only of theoreticians and didacts. The revolutionary credo was one of political activism. The *declassé*, deracinated intellectuals who were to form the nucleus of the elite as tribunes of the proletariat must not only be "ideologized," but also "politicalized"—in a far more sweeping sense than anything imagined by Marx. A unique combination must be attained between ideological expertise and political skill and fidelity.

These considerations prompted the Leninist conception of the Party. The general idea of political parties had become fully developed in the nineteenth century long before Lenin, but his conception of the Party was wholly unique—one must look back to the ruling class in Auguste Comte's "corporate state" for a comparison. Lenin's views were particularly different from the idea of the party as it developed in fascist theory. To the fascists, their Party was to be broad-based, substantially open, indeed, a sort of national movement, ideally embracing all the members of the society not inherently unfit for membership, due to irremediable ethnic or intellectual dispositions. Hitler proposed enrolling in the Nazi Party one out of every ten Germans and he succeeded. Lenin's Party, on the other hand, was to be a tiny, highly exclusive coterie of the fanatically dedicated and ideologically sophisticated.

Nor did Lenin's concept bear any resemblances to the political parties of the constitutionally-grounded states of Europe and America. Lenin's harshly-worded attack on "democratic" institutions and procedures (i.e., popular representation, majoritarianism, the franchise, etc.) reduce finally to one objection: the practices of liberal democracy are, in fact, merely cynical devices of the capitalistic exploiters to keep the working classes docile by giving them the appearance of choice or political participation when, in fact, the only choices provided are between various groups of exploiters, bound together, indeed, in a conspiracy to preserve their exploitive perquisites by the continued enslavement of the workers.

CONTRASTING VIEWS OF THE PARTY

Thus, the Party of Lenin need not trouble itself with how it is to operate in a pluralistic setting; it was to be, itself, the instrument of state direction. Its claim upon this absolute mandate would rest upon its superiority in understanding and interpreting the inexorable march of the dialectic (as Marx had conceived it) and upon its being, presumably, totally benevolent. Marx, in sum, did not say too much about how the state was to be practically governed; he more or less left that to the drift of historical determinism. This notion was a luxury of thought that Lenin did not believe he could afford.

A certain ubiquitous solidarity would seem to be demanded in such an elite and, indeed, in Lenin's view, this is the case, yet he also makes an interesting distinction regarding the grounds of dissent within the Party. He says, in substance, that the social "ends" declared in the official ideology are beyond question, criticism, or debate, but the "means" to those ends are matters appropriately open to discussion and divergence of view. In practice, as has been evidenced in communist regimes, it is often difficult to clearly separate "ends" from "means," but since the Party is internally hierarchical, it must be assumed that there are those who may authoritatively decide what is an "end" and what is a "means."

The party concept, as we will see later, has played a particularly significant role in the development of "bureaucratic theory" in more recent communist thought. The party concept in Lenin's seminal conception, is a direct reflection, via certain organizational modifications, of the principles of dialectical materialism. However, as the idea of the party matured and a "tradition" developed (as in the Soviet Union), the Party structure tended to produce its own internal "norms," apart from the abstractions of Marxist-Leninist philosophy, an essentially bureaucratic phenomenon, described, in theory, by Max Weber.

Marx's general viewpoint was cosmopolitan and anti-nationalistic. He viewed nationalism as a serious threat to the international consolidation of the proletariat. Moreover, he assumed that although the revolution must begin in a given national state, it would quickly spread so as to become an international condition.

Lenin had no such illusions about the simultaneity of revolutionary ferment or the ease with which the nation-state system would topple. His ideas regarding the Party presumed the base of the nation-state. But beyond this, Lenin boldly weds Marx's "class war" hypothesis to the existing nation-state system. He advances the assertion that there are "exploiter" and "exploited" *states* and that the class war is carried on in the realm of international politics. The word *imperialism* is added to the Marxist vocabulary; Lenin uses it to describe the last manifestation of capitalism, the attempt of an expiring economic system to rescue itself by international exploitation.

This outlook, beyond accepting the virtual necessity of the nation-state system, changes the whole concept of the international revolution from the Marxists' beliefs in the virtually simultaneous rising of the proletariats of the advanced industrial nations to Lenin's piece by piece capture of states in a chessboard-like confrontation with the powers of imperialism. Beyond the practical problems of making communism function successfully in one country, Lenin, undoubtedly encouraged by the internationalistic counsel of Leon Trotsky, sought to promote, in his way, the Marxist goal of world revolution. If this were to be accomplished, given Lenin's over-all concept of the international struggle between imperialist and socialist states, revolutions would have to occur under a variety of economic and cultural conditions. This meant, in effect, that the communist revolution, in various places, must be spearheaded by a revolutionary party as against the express types of socio-economic maturation insisted upon by Marx.

Still crucial for Lenin, however, was the revolution as it took place in the advanced industrial states. The Russian Revolution was only a beginning and the revolution developing within the confines of national states must, contended Lenin, be a temporary condition, but, presumably, a lengthy one. Lenin preserves his tie with Marx by accepting Western and Central Europe as the cockpit of the world, so to speak. Trotsky once observed that "the socialist revolution begins on national grounds . . . but it cannot be completed on these grounds."

The on-going ideological development of what was to be designated as "Marxism-Leninism" is seen clearly mirrored in the choices available as Lenin's successor in the Soviet Union: Leon Trotsky, cosmopolitanist, theoretician, ideologist, and European, as against Josef Stalin, nationalist, politician, Oriental. The victory of Stalin in the ensuing internecine contest had the effect of moving away from the ideology of Lenin, creating yet a new metamorphosis in the narrative of Marxist theory. However, Stalin's overtly nationalistic outlook can be traced, in part, to the acceptance of the idea of the nation-state in Lenin's thought.

Stalin's communism was, in actuality, the first example of

"national communism," even though he himself conceived the Soviet Union as an instrument for the accomplishment of the world communist revolution. The means to that end, in Stalinist terms, were the more or less conventional techniques of the Realpolitik, in contrast to classical Marxist concepts. In any case, the "world revolution," sponsored internally in capitalist states or promoted by the expansion of the Soviet "sphere of influence," was secondary to the encouragement of domestic strength and security. For Stalin, the complete triumph of the Party was necessary before all else. The security of the regime became tantamount to the security of society. The industrial sinews of defense must be strengthened. Foremost was Stalin's Slavophilic interest in the East, urged upon him by a number of Bolsheviks convinced of the failure of the revolution in Europe. The sum effect of this Oriental preoccupation was to further decosmopolitanize classical Marxism.

EMERGENCE OF THE COMMUNIST PARTY IN CHINA

With Stalin, two important neo-Marxist variations emerge: (1) the appearance of full-blown statist theories and (2) the reemergence of nationalism. This latter convolution, latent in Leninism, had a particular application to Asia whose cultural configurations were markedly alien to Marxist theory. China, for example, had witnessed its own unique forms of political radicalism dating back to the nineteenth century. Moreover, China had been rent not only by continuous civil strife, but also by many insurrections directed at the crumbling Manchu dynasty. One of these, the revolt of 1912, finally brought a republic into being under Sun Yat-sen. But the rule of the *Kuomintang* (Nationalist People's Party) was insecure, despite its proclamation of "Nationalism, Democracy, and People's Livelihood." It did manage some more stable periods under Bolshevik-educated General Chiang Kai-chek, the "Red General," who was an ex-protégé of Michael Borodin, the ubiquitous Soviet agent in China. Yet vast areas of China suffered under control by regional brigands and the *Kuomintang* claim of ending the institutionalized corruption of the Manchu reign was not entirely justified. The importation of Marxist-Leninist ideas into China, via revived Soviet interest in Asia as a theatre for revolutionary activity, occurred quite early and was widespread.

By 1921, a Chinese Communist Party existed, led by the son of a reasonably prosperous peasant, Mao Tse-tung. From the beginning, Mao represented a strange amalgam of influences—a passionate spirit of Chinese nationalism joined with an intense exposure to the revolutionary literature of Europe, primarily the thoughts of Marx and Lenin.

These influences developed in Mao's mind the vision of a novel form of national revolution, in some respects resting on a conception of the *Volkgeist* reminiscent of the evolution of fascism. Several factors must be taken into account in such a revolutionary outlook. China was a nation overwhelmingly peopled by peasants and small farmers. It lacked any appreciable industrial base. It possessed deeply ingrained and historically static cultural morés. In short, it was the antithesis of the condition thought by Marx to be productive of the revolution brought into being by proletarian self-consciousness.

Mao's revolutionary concept rested upon the emergence of a "national revolutionary spirit," albeit one placed in motion by a minority of the ideologically enlightened. Rejecting Marx's "class warfare" determinants, he conceived of a revolutionary phalanx drawn from all social classes, but predominantly from the oppressed peasantry, who were unified not so much on the basis of economic circumstance, as on the basis of their affirmation of the revolutionary ideology, a doctrine articulated in nationalistic rather than social class commitments.

Mao's movement was, initially, a "peasant movement," exchanging the proletariat for the peasantry on the grounds that China was a peasant nation exploited by imperialist transgressors, a concept that he borrows from Lenin. The struggle between "exploiters" and "exploited" was no longer to be seen, in Mao's eyes, as primarily a contest between economically-determined social classes, but between nations—"proletarian" nations versus "imperialist" nations.

This peasant uprising Mao invests with the rhetoric of mysticism, the ethos of Chinese self-consciousness. He speaks of the "awakening" of the peasantry as a "tempest," a "tornado," an "irresistible wind" that will smash the decaying frame of Chinese life imposed by alien imperialists and their indigenous "running dogs." He makes references to a self-directing will embodied in the militant peasantry and makes the Party the corporal instrument of that will, relegating an elite intelligentsia to a very subordinate role, although as Mao's movement gained prominence and, finally, power, the organizational functions of the Party were noticeably enhanced.

At first glance, this self-directing quality of the peasantry appears similar to Marx's view of the proletariat, but there are notable differences:

1. The sources of this collective self-consciousness can not be directly traced to "conditions of production," but to a far less tangible yearning for "liberation," for breaking the shackles of exploitation, cultural, as well as economic.
2. This self-consciousness is motivated by nationalistic zeal, a desire for national wholeness, the expunging of foreign influences. Indeed, although Mao's view of the human person is couched in very obscure language, it implies a less reductionistic outlook than Marx's. In any case, it is decidedly more emotional and mystic.

In more functional terms, the peasant base (with its allies from various segments of the "class" structure) requires that the strength of the revolution rest in the countryside, with Mao's well-known theory of the "encirclement of the cities" as a ramification. Somewhat like Marx, Mao calls for an eventual eradication of the differences between rural and urban life. However, where Marx basically implies the urbanization of the countryside, Mao urges the imposition of a fundamentally rural or agrarian concept upon the city—the universality of the "commune."

The broad coalition of national groups, founded on the peasant base, imbued with the national spirit, springs into actuality at the time of the Japanese attack on China in 1937. Mao, in response, develops a doctrine that fuses his socio-political revolutionary thesis with a concept of revolutionary tactics, first to be employed against the invading Japanese and later against the forces of the Chinese Nationalist Government. This fusion of political and military doctrine stresses the continuous character of revolution, its virtually perpetual ferment, in contrast to the more systematic historical dialectic of Marxism.

Certain conditions seem to flaw Mao's invocation of the national popular front (in precise Maoist terms: "the peasantry, the working class, the petty bourgeoisie and the national bourgeoisie"). One factor is the inevitable thrusting of the Party into a position of even more expansive power and authority to counter the implicit diversities of the population. This need for positive national identification, quite beyond the more esoterically-phrased explications of the ideological dogma, has resulted in the elevation of Mao himself as a pseudo-divinity (going far beyond the "cult of personality" of the Stalin era). In part, perhaps, the unique talismanic motifs attached to the personage of Mao and his "sacred book" of "living thoughts" is traceable to the latent religiosity of the Oriental. In any event, a sharp contrast can be made between the "government by bureaucracy" image of the current Soviet leadership and the still rampant personalism of the Chinese leadership.

The possession by the Chinese leadership of "universal truth" (a truth of an even more expansive scope than that presumably possessed by a more Marxist-Leninist-oriented elite because it encompasses a less economically-delineated philosophy) results in a more intense "politicalization" of Chinese life. At a time when there are signs of a de-emphasis, however minor, on politicalization in the Soviet Union, the Chinese have increased it. The reasons for this are that given the concept of the on-going or continuous revolution, free from the confines of a strict historical dialectic, the political direction and educational effort of the state become more imperative. Since that revolution in its metamorphosis is less economically-determined, the goals and procedures become more politically-articulated. Historical change is seen as being forged by voluntaristic political action.

Finally, the "liberation" of the Maoists from the rigidities of Marxist dialectic has, as one result, the lack of specific "signposts" along the revolutionary path. Although it is true that specific national objectives are announced by the Chinese, reminiscent of "Five Year Plans" and their equivalents, no other normative criterion can be finally appealed to, other than the somewhat amorphous "national will," requiring, of course, the more precise interpretations of Chairman Mao or those who speak with the authority of the Party.

The world, including the Soviet Union, was startled by the phenomenon of the "Cultural Revolution" of 1968 with its attendant rampages of the Red Guards. It was startling because it was unprecedented in the history of Marxist-Leninist ideology. There had been surprising and even shocking events to be witnessed in post-revolutionary Russia: the elimination of the Kulaks, the purges under Stalin, various Kremlin coup d'état power confrontations, the "secret speech" of Khrushchev. But these were seemingly less bizarre than the unanticipated explosion of political frenzy in China.

The key to understanding this provocative event is the word "cultural." Mao, in order to proceed with his revolution, faced two predicaments altogether foreign to Marxist orientations: (1) the revolution was being undertaken within a national culture especially notable for the continuity and resilience of its ancient social practices; (2) the very segment of the society that formed the revolutionary base, the peasantry, was particularly imbued with these cultural influences, quite in contrast to Marx's proletariat, which developed its self-consciousness, its ideology, as a result of the destruction of its cultural foundations. To these factors may be added one other: the activity of governmental administration invariably, under contemporary conditions, leads to the creation of a bureaucratic hierarchy which, in turn and to varying degrees, develops internalized norms which may, again, be different from or even hostile to the central "master ideal." In the evolution of Soviet communism, this phenomenon has tended to modify the "master ideal," if that is a hasty way of putting it. It was apparent that Mao had no intention of permitting a similar tone of "revisionism."

The Cultural Revolution had a two-sided objective: first, to assert the national will (as embodied in Mao's ideology) against the essentially *cultural* conditions that restrained it, thereby destroying the pre-Maoist cultural base, which implicitly threatened the transference of cultural loyalty to the new institution of the national state, and secondly, to aggressively counter the growth of a bureaucratic superstructure within that state. The result was a premeditated invocation of seemingly spontaneous violence and retribution.

It was, in large part, the temporary restoration of revolutionary terror.

The Cultural Revolution says a good deal about the final character of Maoism and the increasing nationalization of Marxism-Leninism. It emphasizes, among other things, that the nationalization process, in the Chinese manifestation, involves an elemental rejection of Marxist philosophical premises, granted the retention of some Marxist social recommendations. In more specific philosophical terms, it shows, by very vivid and rudimentary political action, the shift away from the materialistic assumptions of Marxist philosophy and the introduction of neo-idealistic elements. Mao himself speaks vaguely of "universal laws" of human existence, invokes quasi-metaphysical categories of "will," "spirit," and "destiny." Indeed, a strange tone of transcendentalism pervades the Maoist testimony. It suggests the idea that revolution-*qua*-revolution may be desirable on its own terms, irrespective of social goals, that the revolutionary society is to be preferred to a stable or tranquil one, that the ultimate social goal may be the preservation of revolutionary fervor and intensity.

All of this is most unlike Karl Marx who believed, with scientific and historical assurance, in the eventual fruition, satisfaction, and homeostasis of society. For him, the society will come to rest upon the total fulfillment of human needs, as he saw them.

NATIONAL COMMUNISM IN OTHER COUNTRIES

The rise of national communism reveals other variations and we might examine the ideological peregrinations involved in the emergence of communism in Cuba, Yugoslavia, and Eastern Europe. In 1957, the Yugoslavian writer, Milovan Djilas predicated that "the leaders of communist parties . . . are driven to experiment with the idea of national communism."

In the period Djilas refers to there were experiments of this sort afoot. This was also the era in which the so-called "Third World" made its presence felt, the term being applied loosely to the ex-colonial countries of Asia and Africa and to certain unaligned states of Europe and South America. Most of these states sought to avoid an explicit Russian- or Chinese-style communism, but most endeavored, also, to steer away from the patterns of the western democracies, revealing some enthusiasm for political radicalism. The types of regimes produced were baffling in their diversity, which reflected the intense nationalistic concerns from which they operated and the conditions of their political origins. Some of these states elected to place themselves broadly within the Marxist-Leninist orbit on a sort of pro forma basis. Two interesting illustrations are Tito's Yugoslavia and Castro's Cuba.

In comparing Yugoslavia and Cuba, one difference is notable: Yugoslavia began as a more or less "orthodox" communist state at the conclusion of World War II and then developed into a society "communist" only in a rhetorical sense. Cuba, following the successful revolution led by Fidel Castro in 1959, became identified with the Marxist-Leninist ideology somewhat as an after-thought. In 1961, Castro publicly referred to himself as a "Marxist-Leninist." Castro was predominantly a nationalist and, broadly, a socialist, and the primary appeal of his movement initially was its vow to overthrow the unpopular government of General Fulgencio Batista and to reduce American influence in Cuba.

In the days of Castro's revolutionary activities and early in his conduct of the control of the government there was little evidence of a doctrinaire ideological posture. Emphasis was placed on the particularity of the Cuban situation. Moreover, the Party did not appear to play as central a role as that envisaged by Lenin. Instead, the élan of the movement was propelled by the camaraderie of the guerrilla formations—leading some commentators, since, to refer to Cuban communism as "guerrilla communism."

However, as the Castro regime, after 1959, extended itself, Castro turned to more ideological considerations. But by embracing Marxism-Leninism, he did, in fact, reject most of the dogma by virtue of his assumption that the Cuban Revolution was wholly unique. One obvious feature of this alleged uniqueness was Castro's attempt to perpetuate the spirit of the guerrilla movement, both internally and externally. The Party—in the Leninistic sense—becomes subservient to the military enthusiasm. The governmental style is shaped by the experience of a partisan army. The ideal is a nation on a virtually perpetual war footing of a popular revolutionary variety, reminiscent of the "wars of liberation" fought in Latin America against colonial control. Like Maoism, Castro's thought implies a continuous revolutionary ferment, and the ideological evolution is less dependent on universal principles and more emphatically on the results of national circumstances.

The concept of communism exhibited by Yugoslavia is yet different. Beginning as a partisan movement against German occupation in World War II, Josip Broz "Tito" sought to establish a state upon the base of a diversified and hostile ethnic population. His first step was to eliminate a competing partisan movement led by Draja Mikhailovic, initially supported by the western powers. In some respects, Tito's conception of the role of the Party suggested a rather orthodox Leninism, but Tito's aspirations were almost entirely nationalistic, particularly in terms of preserving his regime from the threat of internal ethnic fragmentization. His social and economic theories appeared highly eclectic. Moreover, he interpreted the "world communist revolution"—Lenin's theories of the encirclement by the capitalist states—as being, in large part, a facade for more conventional imperialistic ambitions generated by the Soviet Union. Such a view of the Soviet giant prompted Tito to move Yugoslavia into a virtually "neutralist" position in international affairs and even to establish not altogether inharmonious relations with the western alliance.

Internally, the Tito regime moved resolutely away from Marxist-Leninist economic and social policies, incorporating, in some respects, the attitudes of the social democratic movement, albeit under the aegis of a one-party government. Having gone through its period of violence, the Tito regime noticeably softened its political techniques, moving away from the "on-going revolution" concept toward an almost bourgeois solidity, coupled with a growing integration of its nationalistic preoccupations with a greater flexibility and open attitude toward international intercourse. In sum, Yugoslavia embraced a form of state socialism, largely unconnected with Marxist premises and displaying some elements of what might be called "creeping capitalism."

Although Eastern Europe remained, after World War II, definitely within the Soviet sphere of influence, the growth of national communism can be noted here, unrepressed even by Soviet military interventions in Hungary and Czechoslovakia, the latter instance revealing the threat presumed to exist to the Soviet Union by the accelerating process of ideological fragmentization. Five factors appear to contribute to these nationally-articulated reinterpretations of classical communism:

1. The existence of particular national characteristics among the states of Eastern Europe, for example, the ethnic and cultural singularity of a non-Slavic state, such as Romania or the persistence of Catholicism in Poland.
2. The increasing emphasis on private consumption, the desire for economic progress, and its consequent influences on international trade.
3. The inability of "old line" Communist parties to perpetuate a strict ideological uniformity among the young.
4. The presumed moderating nature of Soviet control, as suggested by the less strident policies of the Khrushchev era.
5. The ideological conflict between China and the USSR.

These factors culminated in the appearance of the Dubček government in Czechoslovakia that certainly flirted with a concept of socialism influenced by social democratic ideals. Such an unorthodox "revision" of Marxism-Leninism was sufficient to provoke a military intervention by the Soviets.

But the harshness of the Soviet response to these Czechoslovakian vagaries did not significantly stifle the momentum of national variation. "Old line" regimes in Poland and East Germany vanished, to be replaced by a communist leadership considerably less doctrinaire. The mood of detente was in the air, i.e., the softening of relations between East and West Germany, a state governed in recent years by the Social Democrats. Romania displayed an almost startling disregard for the Soviet Union, even in the hours of the Czech invasion.

REVISIONISTS: A SUMMARY

Such events were reflective of a counter-movement against the Marxist-Leninist orthodoxy, varying in tone from Maoism to cautious experimentation with democratic socialism. This revisionist movement could be sub-divided between one form, which stressed the "infinite" revolution, and another, which sought to modify the primacy of ideology by experimentation with various combinations of social and political doctrine.

This latter tendency could be perceived even in the evolution of Soviet communism. In a sense, the nature of the Party changed from Lenin's original formulation. It did not relinquish its absolute political control and it remained the fountainhead of matters ideological. However, it began to display the characteristics of a state bureaucracy, not overtly different at a primary level from characteristics of bureaucracies in non-communist societies. Such a bureaucratic development usually includes the production of values which are expressly contingent upon the bureaucratic organism, not necessarily an off-spring of ideology. At this level, there may be a conflict between bureaucratic and ideological norms. The dampening of revolutionary zeal provides an opportunity for the birth of these internalized bureaucratic values.

The growth, in the Soviet Union, of such a bureaucratic orientation has been slow, covering several decades, but its presence places the USSR among those states slipping away, in their national experience, from the explicit doctrines of Marx and Lenin. A feature of the Sino-Soviet ideological quarrel is a dispute over which party is true to the principles of Marx and Lenin and the obvious answer is that neither are purists in this ideological sense, both represent various forms of revisionism. To some degree, this confrontation of the communist super-powers represents a clash between the bureaucratic state and the revolutionary state. The fact of the matter is that the bureaucratic state departs from the Marxist model, but the revolutionary state sponsors an idea of revolution severed from a Marxist definition.

The development of the socialism in the nineteenth century that is identifiable with the social democratic movement was somewhat influenced by Marx, far less by Lenin, and almost not at all by post-Leninist communism. In the nineteenth century, there were important socialist movements prior to Marxism (in France, particularly). In Britain, although in point of time the Christian Socialists and, later, the Fabians were mainly post-Marx, they were only distantly impressed by Marxist hypotheses—although there are genteel Marxist nuances in the works of G. B. Shaw, a charter member of the Fabian Society.

The social democrats, in varying degrees, found much virtue in socialism as an economic point of view, but their political and social views were not the direct off-spring of an exclusively economic perspective. Socialism, in the broad usage, can only refer to some concept of public ownership of the means of production, total or partial. In practice, this social democratic conception of socialism, the viewpoint of the non-Marxist Left, approached the socialistic ideal from two premises: (1) the possibility of the attainment of socialism (coupled with social reforms) within the framework of constitutional democracy—a non-revolutionary "gradualism" that stressed conventional political techniques and mass education as the primary means; and (2) a close connection with trade unionism. Such a perspective produced the social democratic parties of Europe, such as the British Labour Party. The Fabian Society, which served as a sort of brains-trust for the British Labour Party, had no equal in terms of their educationistic optimisms. Indeed, their very name implies their gradualistic orientation.

By the time of the post-World War I period, the social democratic momentum had become institutionalized in increasingly successful political parties. They formed the governments in many European parliamentary democracies. One result of this prominence was that this moderate socialistic point of view became even less doctrinaire in terms of economic theory. The socialistic programs of the social democrats (often officially labeled as such, on the continent) became wholly non-Marxist; instead, they favored various concepts of partial "nationalization" of industry, enhancement of public welfare programs, extensions of social egalitarianism and, in short, propelled into being the idea of the "welfare state." This socio-political manifestation reached, perhaps, its most complete expression in Sweden and Denmark, but it also appeared in varying types in Great Britain, Holland, Italy, and Israel. Such a political orientation was also highly influential among the nations emerging from colonial status, such as India.

In the development of this form of socialism, a discrete political philosophy did not emerge, although its economic viewpoints were, in varying degrees, hostile to capitalism. Instead, its explicit political premises were those of the surfacing popular democracy (see chapter six) and, philosophically, the social democrats had long been nurtured by positivism (see chapter five), as can be easily seen in the formative theory of the English Fabians. Indeed, apart from the somewhat bewildering diversity of non-capitalistic economic ideas, this social democratic orientation can be scrutinized under the broad heading of the metamorphosis of popular democracy.

To the emerging "New Left" (discussed in chapter nine), also vigorously anti-capitalistic in the main, Marx represents a venerated father-image, but there is little concrete admiration for "classical" Marxism. In actual political terms, communism was intensely opposed by social democrats, and the revolutionary contemporary New Left has been most extensively criticized by those in the older, social democratic tradition—that might be termed the "Old Left." Indeed, the ideological fideism of the New Left (which it does, of course, inherit from Marxist sources) is particularly unattractive to gradualistic socialists who, granting the adoption of certain, to them, vital economic and social alterations, are content to remain within a society predicated upon democratic pluralism.

The philosophy of revolution (to be considered in another aspect in chapter nine) is no longer explicitly or exclusively communist, except in a loose definition of the term. The schism of the communist world—between nationalistic revolutionaries and nationalistic socialists—represents, at base, a rejection of the fundamental Marxian premise; neither wing now appears to believe in the precept of materialism nor in the dialectical nature of history. The twentieth century has seen the transmutation of Marxism into forms generated by each nation's subjective experience.

FOR ADDITIONAL READING

CASTRO, FIDEL, *Those Who Are Not Revolutionary Fighters Cannot Be Called Communists.* New York: Merit, 1968.

COHN-BENDIT, DANIEL and GABRIEL, *Obsolete Communism: The Left Wing Alternative* (trans. by Arnold Pomerans). New York: McGraw-Hill, 1968.

DRAPER, T., *Castroism: Theory and Practice.* New York: Praeger, 1965.

DJILAS, MILOVAN, *The New Class: An Analysis of the Communist System.* New York: Praeger, 1957.

GREGOR, A. J., *A Survey of Marxism: Problems in Philosophy and the Theory of History.* New York: Random House, 1965.

JACOBS, D. N., *The New Communists.* New York: Harper & Row, 1969.

LAPENNA, I., *State and Law: Soviet and Yugoslav Theory.* New Haven: Yale University Press, 1965.

LENIN, V. I., *What Is to be Done?* Moscow: Foreign Languages Publishing House, 1902.

MAO TSE-TUNG, *On People's Democratic Dictatorship.* Peking: Foreign Language Press, 1949.

MEYER, A. G., *Leninism.* New York: Praeger, 1957.

SCHRAM, S. R., *The Political Thought of Mao Tse-tung.* New York: Praeger, 1963.

TROTSKY, LEON, *The Permanent Revolution* (trans. by Max Schachtman). New York: Pioneer, 1931.

FIVE

The Lodestone of Science

Neo-Positivism

The origins of the philosophical movement called *positivism* can be traced to two related sources: the philosophy of David Hume (and, to a lesser extent, Kant) and a revised conception of science that was characteristic of the nineteenth century. The descent from Hume involves assimilating his anti-metaphysical temper and his radical nominalism; the scientific influence grew from a disinclination to look at the scientific enterprise in speculative terms and rather to deal with it in more expressly problematical terms.

AUGUSTE COMTE

These influences were combined in the thought of the "father" of positivism, who, indeed, coined the word to describe his philosophical outlook: Auguste Comte. Comte, by vocation a mathematician, sought to model the philosophic undertaking on a new definition of science, stressing the description of observable relations between entities encountered in direct experience. His method was primarily empirical and quantitative and he saw philosophy as a sort of "science of science" whose objectives ought to be limited to description as contrasted with explanation and speculation. This descriptive orientation, this cataloguing of the "laws of phenomena," contained a most valuable byproduct: the ability to predict events and, by implication, to control them. Hume's skepticism regarding causality and his "problem of induction" were left behind in this Comtian enthusiasm.

Comte's philosophy exhibits the negative and positive sides of positivism: the rejection of metaphysics and the viability of prediction and control. The culmination of the "positive philosophy" occurs, asserts Comte, as a result of historical progress, what he called "the law of the three stages." The first "stage" he labeled the *theological* and refers to an age in which men conceived of thought in terms of gods, magic, and transcendental phenomena. The second stage was the *metaphysical,* which is but a slight advance, since human thought only replaces the fantasies of theology with the fantasies of metaphysics. Finally, the third stage, the *positive,* features the renunciation of theology and metaphysics and the acceptance of science (as defined by Comte) as the predominant intellectual concern.

The "positive philosophy" was not, for Comte, merely a scientific precept; it was directly applicable to human affairs. A direct off-shoot would be a "science of man" (which, by the way, Comte elected to call "sociology") that could reconstruct human social life. Indeed, Comte was entirely willing to be more specific and draws a utopian picture of a society predicated on the positive philosophy and governed by an elite of scientists in his *System of Positive Polity.*

Comte's sociology strongly resembles a type of "social physics," the identification of "laws" of social action and behavior sufficiently rigorous to allow predictability. Sociology was to be at the top of a hierarchy of supporting sciences of decreasing generality, with mathematics as the base.

Possessed of an intense reformist predilection, Comte enshrines the "positive philosophy" in a "religion of humanity"—a conception that concentrates human proclivities for religiosity into a worship of Humanity, considered as a comprehensive, holistic object, replete with many of the customary facets of religion, including ritual and dogma.

Comte's influence was widespread (although his specific political and pseudo-ecclesiastical preferences were not taken very seriously). J. S. Mill, in England, is a prominent example. In France, his influence can clearly be seen in P. J. Proudhon and in more subtle ways in the sociologists Emile Durkheim and Lucien Levy-Bruhl. In Germany, Ludwig Feuerbach and Ernst Mach contributed varieties of positivistic reinterpretations. Feuerbach expresses succinctly the reductionistic tendencies of positivism by quipping: "Man is what he eats."

The positivism of the nineteenth century strongly stressed five elements:

1. A comprehensive view of the philosophic enterprise as modeled after the orientations of science, particularly physics, denying the credibility of metaphysical and, to some extent, axiological hypotheses.

2. This scientific orientation was largely empirical and quantitative, rejecting scientific argument stemming from arguments to logical necessity. Moreover, positivism in its problematic disposition not only lauded science, but admired the technological applications of science. Its social viewpoint called for amelioration by technological ingenuity; it was, in general, harmonious with the main thrust of the Industrial Revolution —Comte's society was an "industrial society."

3. Positivism's principal trust lay in the predicability of phenomena that it felt would arise from the proper applications of scientific method to the study of human behavior, individual and social. Such delineation of "laws" underpinning behavior and their corresponding predictability provided a base for social planning, and the construction of societies in accordance with this empirical rigor was thought to be altogether attainable by positivism.

4. The positivistic spirit sought to reduce the plethora of data regarding human existence to a reasonably simple set of categories, generally speaking, of a physicalistic sort. This was true not only of positivism's view of nature as a whole, but also of its concept of human nature. Man was to be seen as a purely psycho-biological organism not substantially different from the remainder of the animate species, the lower orders of life themselves being considered as relatively uncomplicated beings.

5. Positivism prided itself on its value neutrality, which corresponded to a defense of ethical relativism. Its ethics could be reduced to a presumably

scientific inquiry into the mechanism of evaluation rather than discourse concerning substantive value.

Nineteenth-century positivism remained, of course, a persistent influence in the twentieth century, particularly, as we will see, in the development of social science. It also provided an indirect influence on other philosophical movements in this century such as *pragmatism* (see chapter six). Within the positivist movement itself, however, certain modifying currents were at work. A basic positivistic orientation prevailed, but the extreme reductionist tendencies were softened. Particularly to be noted was the work of the sociologist, Emile Durkheim, who, while epitomizing positivism's staunch anti-metaphysical attitude, also encompassed a wider-ranging empiricism and exhibited a methodology with a strong rationalistic bent. Durkheim also felt need to acknowledge the moral component in social investigation. Proceeding from rather confined sociological concerns such as suicide (he published a classic treatise on the subject in 1897), Durkheim reached the conclusion that the most serious manifestation in the culture was what he termed *anomie,* a loss of personal identity and social reinforcement that arose from the disintegration of a social hierarchy of values. The concept of anomie, vastly influential in subsequent sociological thought in the current century, clearly defied the nominal categories of positivism. It made reference to a social awareness that could not be adequately expressed by the quantitative methods of conventional positivism. From this concept of anomie, Durkheim also discussed the idea of "collective consciousness," a notion that later intrigued French sociologists and anthropologists, and linked Durkheim to the vitalists, Freud and Jung.

Durkheim has been called a "sophisticated positivist" and there is no doubt that he employed the positivistic vocabulary. He was, also, by his own estimate, an empiricist and a seeker after the rudimentary "laws" of social behavior. Yet his social *Weltanschauung* was broader and richer than the Comtian world-view; he was not a mere physicalist and, indeed, he sought to tread a narrow path between primitive positivism and neo-idealism and, in so doing, to expand the sociology of Comte to include forms of analysis borrowed from anthropology and even history. Unwilling to invoke the super-social mandate of values, he, nonetheless, recognized the insistent phenomenon of value as a vital ingredient in social analysis.

There is a quality about Durkheim that suggests a certain incompleteness in his social synthesis, a disharmony of the affective elements in his thought, but he sketched in unmistakable fashion the vista of a new social scholarship. More than anyone else at the close of the nineteenth century and the beginning of the twentieth (he died in 1917), Durkheim lent credibility to "social science" and stimulated a widespread enthusiasm for a form of social analysis which, although presumably freed from metaphysical bias, sought to account for the full variety of human experience.

NEO-POSITIVISTIC ASPECTS OF WEBER

It can be argued whether or not Max Weber should be connected with the development of positivism. He was not, in a strict sense, a positivist, but his formative influence on the rise of the social sciences cannot be overlooked and the principal thrust of that social science was positivistic.

It is difficult to classify Weber; he was a historian of deserved renown and most assuredly a sociologist in the fuller meaning of that term. Compared with Durkheim, Weber is beset with a wider spectrum of problems, many of them more explicitly political, as is evidenced by his famous theories regarding the rise of the bureaucracy and the charismatic leader.

Aside from Weber's more specific social commentaries (which will be considered momentarily), his major concern was to create a valid method of social analysis; one that would steer clear, simultaneously, of naive positivism and traditional idealism. Its principal characteristic was the introduction into nominal empiricism of a strong emphasis upon conceptualism—the construction of empirically tenable conceptual explanations. This was the method of *Verstehen*—understanding—which was to transcend the level of mere data and narrowly-postulated inductive reasoning.

The neo-positivistic aspect of Weber's thought is evidenced by his belief in the validity of empirically-discoverable "laws" of human behavior and the assumption that these laws were to be predicated upon predicability. Weber was not hesitant, either, to press the argument that these laws could form the basis for normative judgment. Such a viewpoint, Weber's in particular or more generally, rests upon an espousal of causal determinism—the objective consistency of cause-and-effect relationships. The problem for Weber was to explore the question of whether such causality in the natural realm was paralleled by a similar causality in the human environment. Any analysis of cause-and-effect in the natural order differed, at least in one major particular, from a comparable analysis of human behavior: in the latter case, the preconditioning or perspective of the observer must be taken into account—one might easily be "objective" about observing the reproductive habits of fruit flies, but the value-system of the observer must be a factor if the phenomenon under observation is, say, the human sexual morés. Since its beginnings, of course, positivism had emphasized not only the necessity, but also the viability of the objectivity of the social analyst, who was to be compared to the dispassionate natural scientist. Weber does not depart from the thesis that such scientific objectivity is desirable, but he raises the issue of how it is to be obtained, given the historical and ethical conditionings of the observer. Causal explanations, then, must take into account, in a cognitive way, the value predispositions of the observer.

It should be pointed out that Weber only conceived these value predispositions of the observer as an inescapable factor in their analytical outlook and conclusions; the relative degrees of truth or accuracy of these values could not and should not be determined. The recognition of value commitment need not impair the "value neutrality," he argued in sum. Such a perspective had enormous influence on attitudes of the emerging social sciences. Such a contention also raised questions regarding what Karl Mannheim called the "sociology of knowledge." Was there not a certain nominalism or subjectivism in Weber's outlook? If the value predispositions of the observer (his *Verstehen*) were an affective variable in his analysis, then was not this very analysis itself a substantially subjective one? Certainly Weber's basic outlook suggested a nominalistic relationship regarding the significance of phenomena: meaning and significance were given to phenomena by an act of individual human volition. But on this basis, how is one to be sure that one can posit the objectivity of social laws? Is one person's "knowledge" identical, substantially, with another's? Weber assumed that (1) the nature of the object to be investigated predicated a methodological response; and (2) that the value predisposition could be, in a sense, "factored out." This would lead to mutually cognizable concepts, particularly in view of the fact that Weber insisted that all value-judgments, conclusions drawn from investigation, are only relative; they could not present anything other than possibilities.

These elements—and, perhaps, tensions—are revealed in Weber's memorable discussions of bureaucracy. As a social observer, Weber believed he saw in post-Industrial Revolution society the passing of the "old order" in terms of the rise of the modern bureaucratic state, which was thrust into being by a new complex of social values created by the configurations of bureaucratic social organization. The emergence of bureaucracy paralleled the growth of popular democracy, although the express contingency between the two is also implied. Weber is certainly of two minds regarding this advent. Nominally a democrat, Weber took a sanguine view of the eradication of some post-feudal social vestiges brought about by bureaucratization and its potential technological competence, but he was equally alarmed by a possible erosion of freedom that such a metamorphosis suggested. "Value neutralism" was put to a stern test in which Weber's very rationalistic orientations rebelled against the presumed inexorability of the process of bureaucratization.

A similar valuational dilemma was provided by Weber's frequently misunderstood concept of *charisma*. A charismatic quality in a person was not a matter of facile attractiveness or personal magnetism, Weber concluded, but was an "extraordinary quality" that transcends rational appraisal and is akin to magical powers and divine revelations. The claim of the charismatic leader to authority is, thus, the claim of the shaman, the prophet, the leader invested with a superhuman and super-rational dispensation. This quality, Weber tells us, cuts across conventional or customary ideas of social value.

The charismatic leader is the antithesis of the rule of the bureaucracy and such leadership has had an almost immemorial attractiveness, but Weber noticeably recoils from the implications of charismatic authority. The charismatic leader is obviously danger-ous, but only if one cherishes, as Weber evidently did, the idea of the superiority of the pluralistically-constituted society, a society, incidentally, that would seem a virtual requirement for the type of intellectual life Weber expounds. "Value neutralism" and value relativity, as premises, seem to imply, as a social practicality, a pluralistic society. In a curious way, therefore, Weber's theories—and, for that matter, the general posture of positivism—rest upon an implicit moral authority, if only conceived as the necessity for a universal conviction favoring the operation of open and unre-stricted inquiry.

KARL MANNHEIM:
THE OBJECTIVITY OF
KNOWLEDGE

The period between the wars saw the publication, in 1929, of Karl Mannheim's *Ideology and Utopia.* It was Mannheim's clear attempt to rescue rational thought from the assaults of irrationalism—and he had the distinct advantage of being familiar with an intellectual tradition that, by now, included such diverse figures as Marx, Weber, and Freud. Mannheim's position, manifestly appreciative of scien-tific rigor, is markedly skeptical regarding some of the claims of neo-positivism. What he attempted to do was to frame a synthetic interrelationship of knowledge, a new sociological vision, that avoided the implicit suggestion in relativism that knowledge was, finally, wholly subjective and, possibly, illusory. He stresses, likely from a Marxist exposure, the dynamic and even dialectical nature of knowledge that could only be accounted for by assuming the ob-jectivity of knowledge. This "relational" synthesis of knowledge Mannheim rather erratically applies to social analysis, displaying a liking for reformist enthusiasm, utopian speculation and, above all, activistic participation in the historical flow.

POSITIVISM IN THE TWENTIETH CENTURY

The history of positivism in the twentieth century can be best thought of in terms of two main streams: (1) the continuing development of the social sciences, particularly, political science, academic psychology, and sociology, the so-called "behavioral sciences" and (2) the philosophic growth of positivism which took the principal forms of logical positivism and contemporary linguistic philosophy, the two often conjoining.

By the time of the First World War, social science had become a major enterprise. Its principal thrust was to bring to the study of human affairs the same scientific outlook and methodological apparatus that was characteristic of the natural sciences. Its philosophical base was substantially neo-positivistic and its primary tenets could be summarized as follows: (1) a commitment to causal determinism; (2) a rejection of metaphysics and allied ontological analysis; (3) a belief in the feasibility of the discovery of "laws" of human behavior; (4) a dedication to scientific "objectivity"; (5) an empirical and, largely, quantitative methodology; (6) the espousal of value and cultural relativism; (7) an assertion of social atomism; (8) a preference for pluralistic and democratic social organization.

These tenets were expressed in different ways, due, in large measure, to an early abandonment of the idea of a universal "science of man." In psychology, for example, the neo-positivistic orientation took the form of physicalistic theories of stimulus-and-response, as with Pavlov, or the "behavioralism" of John Watson. In sociology, descriptive quantitative analysis predominated. Political study, too, became "behavioral" in the sense that investigation of human behavior was thought to be more pertinent than discussion of more or less abstract principles or institutional analysis. Landmarks in this development were provided in 1908 by the publication of Graham Wallas's *Human Nature in Politics* and Arthur Bentley's *Process of Government*.

To a marked extent, the homeground of positivistically-rooted social science was America, as was evidenced by the work of William James, Mary Follett, John Dewey, and George Herbert Mead.

An important concept that linked to this social theory was

environmentalism. This thesis, at its simplest level, contended that (1) man's nature and his subsequent behavior was largely, if not totally, determined by his experiences in confronting his immediate environment; and (2) prospects for improving human behavior, social relationships, and society in general rested upon "reconstructions" and modifications of his environment as the controlling factor.

This environmentalism took various forms, from Deweyan concepts of education, to sociological theories regarding optimum types of social organization, some of them distinctly utopian in nature. In more general and political terms, the prime concept to emerge was "social engineering" or planned development and control of the environment so as to produce desired modifications in behavior. Such a perspective rested on two considerations: (1) the tenability of the contention that "laws of behavior" could be empirically established; and (2) that it was practical to rearrange the social environment in accordance with these hypothetical models.

This social engineering concept, brought about by social science, differed considerably in scope—from the essentially moderate views of John Dewey to the more fulsome ideas of B. F. Skinner. On the one hand, the resources of social science were seen as a response to more or less explicit social problems, such as crime, poverty, mental illness, or the reform of political institutions. In yet another context, social engineering saw as its object the construction of a model society. The difficulties arose from the fact that although there was a compatibility of philosophical outlook on the part of the "social engineers," they were not at all in agreement concerning the basic origins of human conduct. Being, as positivists, essentially reductionist in outlook, they assumed differing explanations for the root causes of behavior. Thus, such engineering or planning was conceived to be articulated in more or less political, economic, psychological, or social terms, depending on how one viewed the essential nature of man as residing in the realms of the political, economic, psychological, or social. Whether one addressed oneself to pressing social problems or to the production of model societies, the approach tended to emphasize differing cultural instrumentalities. There were, in fact, bitter jurisdictional quarrels among the contending planners.

An interesting variation of this situation is the social theory produced by those who assumed the psychological to be paramount and, hence, the remodeling of the environment ought to be predicated on psychological considerations. Differing approaches can be illustrated by the work of Eric Fromm, especially in *The Sane Society,* who proceeds from a basically neo-Freudian orientation with Marxist overtones, and a work like *Walden II,* written by the behavioral psychologist, B. F. Skinner. More recently Skinner has pressed his arguments for environmentalism against more or less conventional normative ideas in his *Beyond Freedom and Dignity.* One can, indeed, refer to a certain body of literature that advocates what might be termed the "mental health state," as can be illustrated by Herbert Marcuse's *Eros and Civilization* and N. O. Brown's *Life against Death.*

A cleavage can be detected in these efforts, between a concept of environmentalism compatible with the idea of the pluralistic society and those more utopian contentions that advocate more authoritative environmental control and social uniformity. One might contrast the point of view of Elton Mayo, writing between the wars, and the more elitist viewpoints of C. Wright Mills and Herbert Simon of the post-World War II period.

In more concretely political terms, neo-positivist political thought, earlier in the century, tended to disown the uniqueness of politics and to accept a primary reliance on other behavioral areas, such as psychology and sociology. This was partly due to an anxiety regarding the compromising of their objectivity by ideological considerations. Works by Robert McIver, Harold Lasswell, and Seymour Martin Lipset tended to relegate political analysis to sociological or psychological factors. There has been, in consequence, a reaction against the predilection, as is evidenced by the more recent writings of Lasswell.

The on-going problem faced by neo-positivism in the social sciences was the value issue, the framing of some response to the value phenomenon, the same quandary, of course, that troubled Durkheim, Weber, and Mannheim. The Weberian compromise seemed inadequate, especially as the social sciences felt more and more called upon, in the effort of replanning the environment, to make value choices. The mood of activism and reform, never very far submerged under the proclamations of scientific objectivity, demanded some criteria of value.

Neo-positivism's principal response to this challenge has been that judgments regarding value might be made on the basis of empirically sustained "norms." The case has been argued, among others, by David Easton, initially in his *The Political System*. There are two main difficulties in this position, although they may not necessarily be fatal to the argument: (1) the problem of framing normative statements from empirical observation—Hume's problem of the impossibility of deriving "ought" statements from "is" statements; (2) the difficulty in dealing with the problem of the "hierarchy of values."

The first predicament involves the objection that a determination of what *is* is not logically suggestive of what *ought* to be. If one studied a society in which torture was the principal occupation, is one prepared to say on the basis of this discovery that torture *ought* to be the prevailing norm? Of course, it is possible to dismiss this objection as irrelevant and adopt a position of extreme relativism that would simply affirm the existing phenomenon as normative (and *ought* to prevail) solely because those observed norms are those that the people involved evidently select to practice and must be thought to be, for them, entirely satisfactory. But not all neo-positivists are willing to take such a stand, wishing to suggest, instead, that empirically-discoverable "norms" represent a form of consensus that expresses some enduring social value.

But what reason do we have to suppose that this is the case? In any event, this argument implies a regress from a set of norms to some other more rudimentary normative standard. The problem is if the "hierarchy of values" asserts itself. A provocative illustration of this dilemma is provided by the positivistic legal theory of Hans Kelsen. Kelsen, in searching for a normative base for law which is independent of metaphysical conjecture, seeks to find it in human practice, yet in order to sustain these norms, Kelsen is obliged to posit the existence of a fundamental norm, the *Grundnorm,* the "ground norm," to which other norms are related and against which they can be evaluated. But Kelsen is alarmingly vague about the genesis and ontological status of this *Grundnorm.* So, indeed, is a sizeable portion of social science when it confronts the normative issue.

The value problem in neo-positivistic social science is paralleled by its difficulties in resolving the problem of what Plato called the "One and the Many." Given its nominalistic background, neo-positivistic social science initially embraced the position of social atomism—the contention that society can be defined as the sum of its separate parts. It held out against the organicism of European sociology. In a sense, it views society as an artificial construction of human ingenuity comported with an enthusiasm for social engineering; societies, conceivably, could be dismantled and rebuilt at will. Moreover, social atomism fitted well with the individualism characteristic of social science very early in the century. However, the "adjustment" psychology of the pre-World War II era (evidenced in differing ways by both Freud and Dewey) gave way to a more directive hypothesis in which behavioral control seemed far more desirable and practical. As a result, the implicit individualism and pluralism of the Deweyan era, with its emphasis on individual and social interaction, loomed as an impediment to a more radical social psychology. Social theory became more collectivistic and social uniformity more admired; the prospects for social engineering seemed infinitely brighter. Just as the more goal-oriented democratic theorists became more and more suspicious about majoritarianism (see chapter six), social theorists became less and less hospitable to the idea of defining society as a body of discrete individuals.

LOGICAL POSITIVISM

Within philosophy itself, positivism took another direction, toward a viewpoint called *logical positivism*. This term sought to indicate that the basic attitudes of positivism were retained, but primary concentration was placed upon logical analysis, to the point of conceiving philosophy itself as being wholly devoted to this analysis and clarification.

The "headquarters" of this movement was Vienna and is often

referred to as the "Vienna Circle" (made up of such notable philosophers as Carnap, Feigel, and Schlick). Although logical positivism's mode of analysis was broadly mathematical and scientific, initially its view of the function of philosophy differed little from the orientations of the social sciences previously discussed. An example of this wedding of logical positivism and the social sciences can be found in the work of Sir Karl Popper.

But an alteration of this positivistic point of view followed upon the work of Ludwig Wittgenstein, particularly the publication, in 1921, of his *Tractatus-Logico-Philosophicus.* Wittgenstein's influence was strongly felt in Britain, already affected by the philosophies of G. E. Moore and Bertrand Russell and by the publication of the *Principia Mathematica,* authored by Russell and A. N. Whitehead. Wittgenstein's perspective sought to concentrate the logical-analytic propensities of positivism upon *language,* thus bringing into being what is now termed *linguistic analysis* or *language philosophy.*

This shift from natural phenomena to language as the object of the scientific scrutiny of positivism is significant. Early positivism had sought the discovery of laws, but those who followed Wittgenstein had adopted the view that whatever knowledge man possessed, it was contained within language, and, thus, philosophy could only be advanced by an analysis of language and its rigorous clarification. Adherents to language philosophy did divide, however, regarding whether so-called "ordinary" language could be adequately refined to be used for philosophic discourse. Some philosophers argued that "ordinary" language was hopelessly inadequate and that it was vital to produce "ideal" languages of greater precision and clarity, largely based on symbolic language.

It was inferred from this concept that if language was the primary object of philosophic study, then the boundaries of language were also the boundaries of thought. Some more extreme linguistic analysts argued that the "signs" that constitute language have no direct objective referents and, consequently, there is nothing "behind" linguistic symbols, so to speak, no objective meanings. The "meaning" of language, then, results from the signs being invested with meaning by the subjective reception of them by individual men, this reception dependent upon the "emotive" states and conditionings of the person. Denied, in this argument, is the idea that words either enjoy objective meaning or refer to existent entities or categories. Such a conception of the function of philosophy as the clarification of language through the dual method of exhaustive symbolic analysis and the relationship of signs to emotive responses had axiological significance, as, for example, in the ethical writings of Charles Stevenson, for illustration, and in the political analysis of T. D. Weldon and Peter Laslett, among others.

Of especial interest to social thought is one central tenet of linguistic philosophy: the principle of "verification" or "non-falsifiability." This idea rests upon a relatively simple base, familiar to those acquainted with David Hume, the supposition that the meaning of a proposition rests upon its empirical verification and the mode of that verification. Genuine statements or propositions, then, must be statements that can be conclusively verified or "falsified" by empirical means. Such a requirement clearly throws out most of the propositions of philosophy that rely on metaphysical concepts. A proposition such as "God exists" or "knowledge is virtue" is a nonsensical statement, there being no conceivable way to "falsify" such a proposition. And since it is nonsensical, it is also frivolous and irrelevant. The linguistic philosophers were quick to point out that much of the philosophical effort, over the centuries, was devoted to this sort of nonsensical discourse.

But what were the consequences of applying this formula to scientific assertions? The language analysts were not so naive as to assume that contemporary science and its hypotheses proceeded, in fact, solely on the basis of *empirical* verification. The test must be broadened, some argued, to include *logically* possible verification, a position taken, in varying forms, by Popper, A. J. Ayers, and Rudolf Carnap. Ayers, for example, grants the meaning of "analytic propositions"—propositions whose verifiability rests upon internal coherence rather than upon empirical observation.

These tenets of language philosophy were directly applied to political theory by T. D. Weldon in 1953 in his *The Vocabulary of Politics*. Weldon's viewpoint, echoed by others of similar philosophical persuasions, held the conviction that "talk" about politics was not essentially different from any other kind of discourse; one merely uses political language as an object of analysis rather than "talk" concerning ethics or art or religion.

To begin with, Weldon contends that since words (or "signs") represent nothing except what they mean to those encountering them, their meanings being subjectively and emotively fixed, the traditional questions posed by political philosophy are empty rhetoric. Customary discussions of "justice," "right," and the "state" are devoid of meaning, because it was erroneously assumed that these signs referred to some existent and viable abstraction, when, in fact, the only meaning these terms conveyed were the emotive responses they elicited. Consequently, as well, the most frequently encountered propositions in political literature defy any test of verifiability or confirmation. Weldon goes on to assert that the theoretical foundations of democracy, Hegelian idealism, and Marxism are, in these terms, equally flawed.

If this argument is allowed, what function is the political philosopher to perform? Or the student of art, religion, or jurisprudence? The language philosopher replies with an admonition to engage in a blend of psychological and logical analysis which seeks two objectives: (1) a fuller and more complete understanding of the emotive function of language and (2) the further clarification and sharpening of language so as to enhance social communication and to more definitively project alternatives. Indeed, these goals have been pursued by linguistic analysts, not only in political theory, but, also, in art, religion, and jurisprudence, as is evidenced by the writings of I. A. Richards, Anthony Flew, and H. L. A. Hart.

THE WANING OF POSITIVISM

By the 1960s, the influence of positivism appeared on the wane. The linguistic philosophers had had their say and had doubtless contributed to the precision of social discourse. But even in the bastion of linguistic analysis, Britain, the reappearance of more speculative philosophy is beginning to be seen. The Europeans, never intensely enthusiastic about positivism anyway, continue to be preoccupied with varieties of phenomenology and neo-realism. Perhaps, in a more popular sense, the social theory of language analysis was too opaque, too esoterically committed to a philosophy of the "closed room" to withstand the insistent demands brought into being by the tremendous cultural dislocations of the century. Whatever one might wish to say about the validity of, say, Weldon's observations, they do not tell one very much about how to keep the polity from falling apart, except, perhaps, to have a presumably more sophisticated appreciation of the inherent pitfalls of political language.

American social science of a positivistic stamp is also in a slow decline, resulting, in part, from the angry attacks upon it by the new social radicalism with its intensely moralistic fervor (see chapter nine). On a less sociological basis, the diminishing influence of neo-positivism may be the result of two factors: (1) a very searching criticism of its pretensions to scientific objectivity and value neutrality and (2) the inadequacy of its scientific base.

The first factor involves allegations that, in fact, the objectivity of neo-positivistic social science is a disingenuous cover for an ideological bias. In sum, it has produced a social outlook remarkably dogmatic in a philosophical sense and such dogmatism is hardly compatible with its expressed admiration for empirical spirit. Such criticisms have been leveled by many, but some of the more trenchant have been provided by the American political philosopher, Leo Strauss.

The charge is made that the covert social dogmatism of the neo-positivistic social scientists is, in reality, a defense of popular bourgeois democracy—which does not ingratiate them with either the new radicals or the social conservatives. Neo-positivists have defended democracy in philosophic terms, such as Charles Frankel in *The Democratic Prospect*; there is no doubt that positivistic social science embraces fundamental convictions similar to those of popular democracy (e.g., egalitarianism, ethical relativism, belief in progress, et al.) and it traces its intellectual origins in the nineteenth century from common sources. It is not this explicit preference that may be damaging to the credibility of contemporary neo-positivism. Other factors are more significant:

1. Its unwillingness to acknowledge that it does, in fact, espouse a broad social doctrine, with the attendant difficulty that it fails to offer an explicit defense of its viewpoint in these terms.

2. Its lack of appreciation of the contentious nature of most of the basic philosophical premises that underpin its social recommendations.

3. Its almost stubborn unwillingness to engage in serious ethical controversy.

Of these three, the last is the most threatening to neo-positivism's social influence. A. J. Ayers, in his *Language, Truth and Logic,* tries to anticipate the objection that his anti-metaphysical position is, in fact, a counter-metaphysic, simply a substituting of one metaphysical *Weltanschauung* for another. To be candid, Ayers's answer to this anticipated objection is not very convincing. To allege that one is "neutral" in matters metaphysical (or ethical), to say nothing of the contention that one rejects the validity of metaphysical or ethical reflection in toto, does seem to inexorably place one in the position of making judgments relevant to these concerns.

Neo-positivism's ethical neutrality is, in fact, a fairly explicit exposition of an ethical viewpoint. It does promote a concept of value, even if it restricts itself to a discussion of the mechanics of value. Regardless of the merits of neo-positivistic social science's ethical preferences, there is an obvious connection between its concept of what is "good" and "bad," and the social recommendations it chooses to make. It cannot, in all fairness, rest those recommendations, whatever they may be, wholly on an appeal to the authority of its alleged scientific discernment and probity. To do so is to commit the act its critics accuse it of: the introduction of comprehensive value-judgments under the guise of scientific inevitability.

The possible inadequacy of contemporary positivism's scientific base is even more formidable an objection. It is suggested by some that the "science" upon which social science currently operates is the science of the nineteenth century, that its handbook is still Mill's *Canons of Induction,* and the difficulties faced by neo-positivism arise from an insufficient understanding of contemporary scientific thought. More specifically, the philosophical foundations of contemporary science include three major elements, all of which are overlooked by neo-positivistic social science:

1. That there is no *one* correct way to conceptualize the universe—the rejection of what Milton Munitz has called the "one-shot theory of the universe." Science is a matter of entertaining a virtual infinity of possible concepts, the evaluation of which depends upon the coherence and usefulness of the concept rather than upon its "truth" in terms of its replication of an objective and discernible "grand design."

2. The abandonment of a "correspondence theory of truth" and its replacement with a "coherence theory of truth."

3. The acceptance of the validity of demonstrations based upon logical necessity as well as empirical confirmation.

It can be contended that contemporary social science has neglected to take into account the ramifications of these cardinal tenets of science, electing to follow the patterns set by the natural sciences of the last century. The current explosion of scientific knowledge, especially in biology, genetics, and neurophysiology, has, in particular, gone more or less unexamined by contemporary social science primarily for two reasons: (1) the employment by these areas of scientific inquiry of methodologies alien to the social sciences and (2) the implicit philosophical inferences that follow from these investigations strike at the philosophical preferences of positivism. In fact, a new social science seems well on the way to a development that may challenge the hegemony of more traditional social science.

In more directly political terms, neo-positivistic social science has, in very recent times, gone avowedly to the defense of democratic theory (see chapter six). It has paid a certain price for this activist stance. It has re-emphasized its long-standing preference for a neo-Platonic vision of a scientifically-postulated society, managed by the technically competent. This elitist reinforcement of democracy, however, leads to a profound encounter: the historical conviction of democracy that the individual alone has the final knowledge of what constitutes his own best interests is ranged against the view of neo-positivism that men must be conditioned behaviorally for their own good by those who enjoy the benefit of an increased scientific and normative knowledge. B. F. Skinner is, from this latter point of view, quite consistent in proclaiming the obsolescence of "freedom" and "dignity," along with a host of awkward subjective inclinations.

But the tenability of this viewpoint rests upon the demonstration of a scientific authority beyond, if you will, "reasonable doubt." It may well be that the final conclusion of science in the twentieth century will not involve the explicit enunciation of social laws, but, rather, the construction of naturalistic limitations, parameters between which human choice and judgment must operate. Consequently, we are still faced with the problem of determining on what basis those choices and judgments will be made.

FOR ADDITIONAL READING

AYERS, A. J., *Language, Truth and Logic*. New York: Dover, n.d.

DURKHEIM, EMILE, *The Rules of Sociological Method*. Chicago: University of Chicago Press, 1938.

EULAU, HEINZ, *The Behavioral Persuasion in Politics*. New York: Random House, 1964.

GELLNER, ERNEST, *Words and Things*. London: Gollancz, 1959.

MANNHEIM, KARL, *Ideology and Utopia*. New York: Harcourt, Brace & World, 1936.

MATSON, F. W., *The Broken Image*. New York: Braziller, 1964.

NAGEL, ERNEST, *The Structure of Science*. New York: Harcourt, Brace & World, 1961.

POPPER, KARL, *The Poverty of Historicism*. London: Routledge & Kegan Paul, 1961.

SKINNER, B. F., *Beyond Freedom and Dignity*. New York: Knopf, 1971.

VAN DYKE, VERNON, *Political Science: A Philosophical Analysis*. London: Stevens & Sons, 1960.

WEBER, MAX, *The Theory of Social and Economic Organization* (trans. by A. M. Henderson and Talcott Parsons). New York: Free Press, 1965.

WELDON, T. D., *The Vocabulary of Politics*. London: Penguin Books, 1953.

SIX

The Common Man's Century

Popular Democracy

How far back does one have to go to find the roots of democracy? There is Periclean Athens to recall or the religious egalitarianism of the Reformation or the English radicalisms of the seventeenth century or the natural rights theory of Locke or the romanticism of Rousseau or, indeed, the manifestoes of the American Founding Fathers.

If one examines twentieth century democracy in somewhat cautious philosophical terms, it is unnecessary and possibly confusing to trace democratic thought back to the Greek *demos* or even, perhaps, to the republicanism of John Locke. Twentieth century democracy does appear as the off-spring of the nineteenth century, concerned as it is with a concept of social democracy in contrast to the juristic formulations of the Enlightenment. Contemporary democracy is the product—some say the step-child—of a nineteenth century phenomenon called "liberalism." Twentieth century democracy—"popular democracy"—cannot be divorced from the philosophical momentum stimulated by the cultural changes of the last century.

This is not to say that a certain skein of development is not visible. Hobbes, in the seventeenth century, built a certain psychological basis for the philosophy of popular democracy; Hume provided it with the groundwork of an ethic. Rousseau gave it its quasi-mystical coloring. But these currents culminate in the liberalism of the middle of the nineteenth century.

DEMOCRACY AS A MIDDLE CLASS POLITICAL THEORY

It is not customarily said, but democracy is a middle class political philosophy; it is the political theory of the bourgeoisie. Its core is *appetition* and its appearance as a dominant political world-view parallels the social pre-eminence of the middle classes whose internal orientations and values were fundamentally acquisitive, materially and psychologically. The rise to political control of the middle classes grew out of what C. B. McPherson has termed the "possessive individualism" of Hobbes and Locke.

The primary distinction between the democracy of the nineteenth century and that of the twentieth can be discovered in the expansion of those political tenets operationally useful to the middle classes to a fuller range of the society. Uniformity, which is ultimately a marked characteristic of popular democracy, consisted of the successful spread of the middle class ethos to other segments of society, decisively shaping the character of the culture, not only in political but also in ethical and artistic terms. Normative definitions in the twentieth century remain definitions predicated on appetitive assumptions.

The key concept underlying both "classical" liberalism and contemporary popular democracy is, thus, *appetite,* the satisfaction of subjectively felt needs and desires. Throughout the nineteenth century and much of the twentieth, this appetition concerned material or political possessions—thus, capitalism was the altogether appropriate economic expression of this preoccupation—but, more contemporaneously, the emphasis has shifted to psychological appetition, which, fundamentally, lies close to the problem of social (as against legal or political) equality. The crux of twentieth century popular democracy turns upon the emergence of ego psychology, as we shall see.

Problems of definition exist regarding "democracy," divided between those who insist that democracy must be thought of as a body of cognate philosophical principles and those who wish to define democracy as only agreements concerning procedures. But regardless of the definition one selects, the most elemental consideration remains the nature of *human equality*—again, whether one considers equality to be substantive or a procedural desirability.

The most rudimentary explanation of human equality—significant in contemporary democratic thought—is the equality of appetites, a concept rather fully explored by Hobbes. One can argue that although men differ (in, say, strength or fleetness of foot), these differences are inconsequential because men equally seek survival, sustenance, and gratification. Popular democracy— the democracy of our century—begins with the announcement of the equality of desires, first fully proclaimed by Jeremy Bentham.

Bentham's extreme ethical relativism—the "calculus of pleasure"—survived J. S. Mill's attempt to modify it by the introduction of "qualitative" differentiations of pleasure (as Mill presents, curiously enough, an argument to historical authority). While Bentham's ethics were not always triumphant (consider the failure to supersede the English Common Law), they were immensely influential in social theory, and they formed the base for the ethics of American pragmatism, which, in turn, had an intense impact on converting nineteenth century democratic theory into the more popular manifestations of the twentieth.

At one level, the ethics of John Dewey did not depart from the ethics of Bentham: for both, there was no valid means for establishing a hierarchy of values apart from subjective espousal. Deweyan ethics incorporated the idea of "intelligence" as a human capacity provoked by problematic situations, ethical and otherwise. For Dewey, the efficient harmonization of "ends" and "means," by the instrument of intelligence, was the essential moral function, but, in this sense, moral decisions and judgments were not different from any other intelligent resolution of a problematic situation.

The concept that desires are qualitatively equal and self-justifying is not only central to twentieth century democracy's view of equality, but also to its entire social outlook. Regardless of distinctions between substantive and procedural definitions of democracy, the literature of democratic theory in this century has proceeded from this ethical assumption. Only by denying the objectivity of moral truth can other conventional democratic axioms be sustained, among them equality, consent, and majoritarianism. Some Christian theorists, like René deVisme Williamson and John Hallowell, have attempted to argue, substantively, that democratic principles are directly derivable from Judeo-Christian ethics. Their position is fraught with philosophical difficulties, not the least of which is the obligation to show how religious eschatology is reconcilable with the relativistic, appetitive foundations of popular democratic thought.

PSYCHOLOGISTICS OF DEMOCRATIC THEORY

Contemporary democratic theory's defense of human equality, from this ethical purview, is psychologistic. Its principal claim is that no significant qualitative differences exist among men based upon a psychological understanding of them. Differences of view arise, among democrats, not so much from arguments regarding intrinsic notions of equality, but rather from disagreements concerning forms of procedural equality, how "ought" people to be treated from an egalitarianist standpoint. The nineteenth century viewpoint stated that while no impediments to opportunity should exist, individuals ought to be generally entitled to the rewards of their industry, talent, or foresight. The issue turns on the problem of "distributive justice," because a concept of human equality, per se, does not necessarily infer an equality of rewards or even an equality of status based on social performance.

The nineteenth century view, social Darwinistic in mood, is challenged by a twentieth century perspective that emphasizes an enforced equality in the distribution of social advantages and prerogatives. It is this premise that underlies the concept of "participatory democracy," a fashionable phrase in the post-World War II period. Equality in participation, political, economic, and social, is something quite distinct from a more rudimentary equality that is defined as an equal chance at social and economic mobility, granted the equality of legal protection and the opportunity to participate in the formulation of political majorities.

The concept of equality in a distributive sense has developed in three major stages. The first stage exhibited an effort to eliminate any innate or formal disabilities (such as ethnic origins or religion) that would prevent equal access to the competition for social rewards. The second stage sought to limit that competition, not by an imposed, over-all distributive equality, but by limiting the spectrum of social rewards by setting minimum conditions, publically subsidized at one end of that spectrum (e.g., "guaranteed annual wage," subsidized housing, medical services, and welfare benefits) and limiting reward at the other end (high graduated income taxes, confiscation of inherited wealth, restriction on forms of social exclusion). This second stage is identified with what has been called the "welfare state." The third stage involves a comprehensive leveling of social rewards, so as to make operative a general uniformity by the virtual elimination of social and economic competition. The western democracies generally have assented to the rationale of the second stage, but, at present, the desirabilities of the third stage are in great dispute.

The transition in democratic thought from the individualism of the nineteenth century to the collectivism of the twentieth involves differing ideas regarding the desirability of pluralism, the concept that the best society is characterized by tolerance, variety, and a high level of respect for individual differences and preferences. The democracy of the nineteenth century—stage one—was vigorously pluralistic; the democracy of the twentieth century—stage two—manifests a mixed mind on the subject.

THE EMERGENCE OF PRAGMATISM

This changing attitude toward pluralism (and the somewhat eclectic mood that still prevails) can be illustrated in terms of the appearance of an important factor in twentieth century democratic thought: *pragmatism.* The pragmatic movement in philosophy is an essentially American phenomenon, although the British philosopher, F. S. C. Schiller is sometimes referred to as a pragmatist. It originates in the nineteenth century, but becomes prominent after World War I. The work of Charles Sanders Peirce is generally cited as the seminal effort, although it was William James, the American psychologist, who, under Peirce's influence, brought pragmatism into public notice. Also, the "Chicago School," surrounding John Dewey, was an important current—although Dewey himself preferred the label *instrumentalism.*

While the initial concern of pragmatism was clarification by use of scientific and experimental techniques (not unlike positivism with which it is allied), its main argument rested on a concept of truth in which utility, subjectivism, nominalism, and relativism were cardinal elements. The "truth" of judgments and beliefs were thought to rest on their practical consequences, these consequences being defined in terms of workability, individual satisfaction and, presumably, desirable social attitudes.

This definition of truth implied a "reconstruction in philosophy," a rejection of intellectualism in favor of an exclusive attention to a variety of empirically-perceived psychological relationships; it placed strong emphasis on "problem solving" as the universal enterprise, but these "problems" and "solutions" were conceived of in terms of immediate, self-identified human concerns.

In social terms, pragmatism, besides endorsing a sweeping relativism in ethics and anthropology, attacked any assertion of an objective authority, stressing, instead, the resolution of felt desires. Dewey's "self interest theory of value" argued, for example, that the ethical problem could be reduced to a reconciliation of "ends" and "means" by the intervention of "intelligence"—with neither "ends" nor "means" susceptible to normative judgment except in subjective terms. Such a viewpoint was not only anti-autocratic, but also vigorously pluralistic even when softened by Dewey's conviction that, generally, men were disposed toward altruistic social cooperation.

One need only examine the primary tenets of twentieth century democratic thought to see the fine hand of pragmatism. Even nineteenth century democratic axioms become rephrased in pragmatic language. Consider these rather general democratic precepts customarily espoused, at least prior to World War II:

1. Majoritarianism: pragmatic concepts extended this principle to a wide range of human groups.
2. Popular sovereignty: pragmatic influences stressed government as essentially responsive to human problems and needs.
3. Popular representation: pragmatism endorsed an equilibriumist view of the tension between interests.
4. Human equality: pragmatism reinforced a psychologistic view.
5. Legalism: pragmatism encouraged judicial positivism.
6. Individual liberty: pragmatic definitions were subjectivistic, but sought to reconcile social utility with individual prerogative.
7. Value relativism: the pragmatic impact was to press relativism to more radical formulations.
8. Human nature was seen as fundamentally good and improvable.
9. Altruism: in part, defended by pragmatic psychology.
10. Freedom: defined by pragmatism in terms of the positive desirability of unrestricted individual and social experimentalism as necessary to social well-being, provided no authoritarian consequences.
11. First truth: since truth, as defined by pragmatism, rests upon "facts" rather than "ideas," it will prevail without authoritative invocation or protection.
12. Second truth: on the basis of the same definition, truth is that which solves problems.

There are two somewhat curious aspects to this intimate association between pragmatism and democratic theory: (1) from a strictly philosophical standpoint, pragmatism was highly vulnerable to devastating analytical criticism, but this critique largely failed to impair its influences on democratic thought; (2) as a philosophical movement, pragmatism's ascendancy was remarkably short-lived, yet, again, its impact on democracy was far longer-lasting.

THE ENCOUNTER OF THE PLURALISTS
AND THE ELITISTS

Providing, in a sense, a philosophical underpinning to democratic theory, pragmatism's implicit defense of pluralism came under heavy attack at the close of World War II, not only by "anti-democrats," but also by rival democratic theoreticians. One can justifiably use the broad issue of pluralism as the pivotal issue upon which this theoretical confrontation took place. The encounter involves those who we will call *pluralists* against their critics, who we might label as *revisionists* or *elitists*.

The rise of the elitists, in democratic theory, can be traced to their accelerating pessimism regarding the viability of defending democracy in more or less conventional terms. In one sense, they were sensitive to the probing attacks made on democracy, per se, by conservative critics, on the one hand, and by doctrinaire radicals, on the other. But the principal genesis of their ideas is found in their independent conclusion that pluralistic democratic theory is dangerously vulnerable to hard-headed analysis. It was possibly ironic that social science, allowing for its democratic and pluralistic preferences, refined its empirical methods to the point that it began to disclose data chillingly discouraging to nominal democratic optimism. The political interests and capacities of the "common man," as suggested by empirical findings, did not seem reconcilable with the sanguine estimations of democratic apologists; democratic procedures, when studied in depth, did not appear truly "democratic," at least in terms of conventional definitions. In sum, democracy, as popularly imagined, did not seem to work along the supposed lines. One was faced with either admitting that democracy was illusory, as some anti-democrats had long contended, or adopting a different conception of it. The elitists chose the latter position, although they called into play, in their defense of democracy, some theoretical arguments not customarily identified with democracy, borrowed, with modifications, from the elitist European sociologists, Pareto, Michels, and Mosca.

The crux of this new democratic defense inaugurated by the elitists was that the "values" or "rules of the game" of democracy were sound enough, but that, realistically, democracies operate on the basis of elites (as, perhaps, do all social groups, some contended) in contrast to the notion that democracy's nature requires the acceptance of the concept of popular or mass initiative and control. In essence, the elitists wished to argue two main propositions:

1. All political societies operate on the basis of elite control and respond to elite competition (as in Pareto's theory of the "circulation of elites").

2. In a democracy, this competition between elites assumes the form of competition between "democratic elites," defined as those elites that recognize the democratic "rules of the game" and may also espouse, as a part of their elite creed, a devotion to democratic values.

The advantage of this concept, the elitists argue, is two-fold: it is more "realistic," it comports with what actually appears to take place, socially and politically, and it takes into account the important contribution to be made to the maintenance of democracy by specialized and particularly competent elites.

Beyond these general considerations, the elitists adopt differing viewpoints—as is true, of course, with the pluralists. Perhaps it would be useful to briefly examine four examples of the elitist democratic theory, the ideas of Joseph Schumpeter, Robert Dahl, Giovanni Sartori, and Harold Lasswell. In like fashion, we will look at four pluralists for contrast: John Dewey, Joseph Tussman, Henry Kariel and Peter Bachrach. For further contrast, the viewpoints of two more radical democratic theorists, Christian Bay and Kenneth Megill, will be surveyed.

JOSEPH SCHUMPETER

By all odds, the earliest statement of the elitist position is provided by Joseph A. Schumpeter in 1942 in his book, *Capitalism, Socialism and Democracy.* Schumpeter's argument separates the "will of the people" from the "objects" of that will which are "sanctioned by utilitarian reason." The pursuance of these "objects" requires a division of labor in which specialized segments of the society, although in the broadest sense responsible to the public will, must devise the explicit means for articulating and securing these social goals. These goals cannot arise from some adumbrated "common good" since it is impossible to forge an agreement or consensus regarding it and it would, in any case, lack logical sanction.

Schumpeter applies this concept to a definition: "The democratic method is that of institutional arrangement for arriving at political decisions in which individuals acquire power to decide by means of a competitive struggle for the people's vote."

The implications of the definition are clear enough. The "democratic process" is thought to exist in a competitive situation, open to public preferences, by which individuals (and, presumably, groups of individuals) gain the opportunity to make decisions. There is no suggestion that (1) an explicit judgmental criterion exists for those decisions (except the goals sanctioned by "utilitarian reason") or (2) that those decisions correspond to the popular will or (3) that there is involved any notion of popular accountability. Democracy, for Schumpeter, is a device for providing leadership, a device presumably superior to alternative devices, its elemental difference being the "competitive struggle for the people's vote."

He offers a number of defenses for this implicitly elitist definition. Among them are the presentation of a reliable criterion for identifying democratic governments, a forthright recognition of the leadership requirement, a more comprehensive recognition of the clash of interests, a more flexible view of the nature of individual freedom, a more direct means of rejecting leadership and the avoidance of the complex problems of majoritarianism.

ROBERT DAHL AND GIOVANNI SARTORI

Schumpeter's early formulation seems tentative and cursory compared to the more elegant theoretical frameworks of Robert Dahl and Giovanni Sartori. Both Dahl and Sartori introduce a new term: *polyarchy*. Dahl suggests that polyarchy might serve as a replacement term for democracy; Sartori defines democracy by making it virtually synonymous with polyarchy.

The term *polyarchy* appears in response to the thesis that political control is control by minorities. Polyarchy is a political system characterized by a reasonably free and mobile competition between influential and policy-framing minorities. The concept of polyarchy as democracy is contained, in Dahl's case, in his *Preface to Democratic Theory* (1956), *Who Governs?* (1961), and *Polyarchy* (1971). Sartori's version is to be found in his *Democratic Theory*, published in English in 1965.

For Dahl, the problem of democratic egalitarianism can be put this way: (1) equality as a general principle is desirable and (2) most of the conventional forms of inequality can be successfully adjusted by social action (e.g., matters of wealth, elementary political rights, and certain forms of social status). Indeed, the effects of progressive democracy in the twentieth century tend to illustrate the success of this form of egalitarianism. Such have been the accomplishments of what Dahl calls *populistic democracy.*

However, populistic democracy has not been totally successful in realizing the egalitarian ideal nor has its procedures been adaptable to the size and complexity of huge industrialized societies. There are other factors, Dahl discovers, that inhibit the attainment of the egalitarian ideal. There exist sharp differences in motivation to participate or to acquire power, different intensities of influence and reception of information. Some citizens in the democracy belong to influential policy-determining groups or are the direct recipients of such influences. In fact, if one is realistic, argues Dahl, both in terms of participation and the distribution of power and weight of influence, the political structure, operationally, is best analyzed in terms of highly influential groups who, in fact, control and direct the mechanism of political power. To these groups and their activities Dahl has affixed the term polyarchy.

These democratic polyarchies are not, for Dahl, little oligarchies. As a matter of fact, he refers to "egalitarian polyarchies." The problem of enhancing participation—realizing the aim of egalitarianism—involves not the conventional cross-societal norms regarding participation, but, rather, opportunities to participate via participation in polyarchies, to have access to the instrumentalities of decision formulation. Not the least of these capabilities would be the evaluation and selection of these polyarchies, as Dahl conceives them as being competitive and immersed in dynamic process. This conception of a political order, based essentially on an equal opportunity to participate in the elitist sub-structure of the society, Dahl calls *polyarchal democracy.*

Dahl's explicit distinction between democracy and dictatorship does not rest on a difference between government by majority and government by minority. The distinction comes much closer to being between government by *a* minority, as against government by minorities. Indeed, Dahl's democratic theory, while elitist, rests upon a pluralism of elites, where the sheer number of elites, as well as their diversity, becomes an important factor.

Also, Dahl's theory is equilibriumistic; that is, it finally rests, as an anti-autocratic alternative, upon a predictable balancing of interests and social forces. He expresses this faith in equilibrium in a number of ways, among them being the supposition that the protection against tyrannical, oligarchic usurpation arises not from constitutional checks, but from the competition or "balancing" of elites or polyarchies. Moreover, there is a clear suggestion in Dahl that the spectrum of polyarchies will be representative of the major configurations of the society, as pertaining to social classes, ethnic and religious groupings, age patterns and so on, thus achieving a kind of representative consensus through the operation of polyarchies.

Another interesting presentation of the elitist position is provided by the Italian theorist, Giovanni Sartori, in his comprehensive analysis of the theoretical base of democracy entitled *Democratic Theory.* If Dahl's perspective is a blend of neo-positivism (as is evidenced, if in no other way, by his disinterest in the question of the normative claims of competing elites) and the Paretian school of sociology, Sartori is far more a historicist, a continental "liberal" recalling Toqueville, who is far more skeptical about the egalitarian ideal than Dahl.

While Sartori accepts the premise that democracy is concerned only with the right to choose and does not imply a value criterion for choice, he also insists that the quantitative procedures of democracy have a qualitative objective. He strongly criticizes a tendency of overquantified democratic procedure—the "law of numbers"—to the point where a severe deterioration of leadership occurs. Somewhat like Schumpeter, Sartori deems leadership production the primary democratic function.

Sartori describes democracy as an *elective polyarchy.* He calls it "elective" to contrast it with systems not based on popular suffrage; non-elective polyarchies contain no reliable control of leadership. "Democracy," states Sartori, "is a political system in which *the influence of the majority is assured by elective and competitive minorities to whom it is entrusted.*"

The merit of this definition, Sartori contends, is that it emphasizes that political control not only rests with citizens, but also with contending leaders and it implies that minorities are the imperative element in the system. Sartori recognizes, however, that this definition, this conception, does not touch upon the qualitative problem of leadership. He remains content with the assumption that competing, elected minorities will invariably produce a leadership of sufficient quality to meet democratic requirements.

Sartori defends his conception of democracy in two ways, saying (1) that it does not discard the "classical" theory of popular mandate, but completes it and (2) that it expresses a proper distinction between "scientific exactness" and "ideocratic value," especially in regard to the prejudice against elites. Sartori concludes that the task is to conceive of a political community with leadership, but one in which coercion gives way to inducement.

HAROLD LASSWELL

The last of our brief examples of contemporary democratic elitists is Harold Lasswell. Lasswell might well be considered in the chapter on neo-positivism. His personal intellectual hegira has taken him through a series of preoccupations, from power theory to positivism to interests in the implications of depth psychology to political elitism. In Lasswell, the concept of the elite wavers between the polyarchal perspective and a more overt enthusiasm for a scientific or technocratic elite.

This latter emphasis is rooted in three contentions: (1) that the elite must be presumed to be recruited from the society at large; (2) that the leadership of society should be founded upon a scientific approach to policy-making; and (3) that the fundamental problem of democracy is "to improve the layman's judgment in selecting expert advisers and guides," to evaluate, in other words, what Lasswell likes to call the practitioners of "policy science."

While Lasswell's theories regarding elites have undergone some changes—shifting, one might say, from normative to operational definitions and back again—his principal contribution to contemporary elitist thought has been his emphasis on the manipulative functions and capabilities of elites (as the necessary instrumentalities for the furtherance of democratic postulates). Evident throughout Lasswell's most recent thought is the neo-Platonic notion of elite leadership as engaging in social therapy, ministering to the ills of the body politic, often in expressly social psychiatric terms. It is in this spirit that Lasswell speaks of "preventative politics." He contends that "democratic theorists in particular have hastily assumed that social harmony depends on discussion, and that discussion depends upon the formal consultation of all those affected by social policies." He advocates a direct attack on social "pathologies" by the application of the "preventive medicine" of scientifically-postulated "policy." Lasswell's social psychiatry presupposes some rather sweeping modifications of conventional political techniques and the reconstitution of social institutions. These modifications have a common thrust: to both equalize and minimize the use of power in society. Power is viewed as the primary cause of the tensions and anxieties that produce widespread psychological maladies. He proposes, therefore, a radical egalitarianizing of social institutions and political processes with the objective of the virtual extermination of power. It is somewhat paradoxical, however, that Lasswell seeks to limit or abolish power by means of expansive exercises of it, in order to support the coercive aspects of "preventive politics."

Moving much further away from nominal pluralistic orientations than Dahl and Sartori, Lasswell's manipulatory concepts have been described as propagandistic. His concept of the role of elite leadership developed from the objective of the "clarification of goals" to bringing about "positive realignments of behavior" by "overt acts" of social reconstruction. Emergent was a more explicit qualitative concept of the elite or elites and the requisite authority and legitimacy that their especial capabilities introduced. This avowedly manipulatory rationale, this rule by scientific elites, was thought to be, by Lasswell, a transitional phase, a bridge to a utopian democracy, the main feature of which would be the retirement of power as the primary characteristic of political life. "It should not be denied," argues Lasswell, "that the long run aim of societies aspiring toward human freedom is to get rid of power and to bring into existence a free man's commonwealth in which coercion is neither threatened, applied, nor desired."

Lasswell's version of this attainable society is provocative, because it discloses the "values" which must be thought of as being fundamental to the democratic goals, which the "policy sciences" seek to maintain and realize. These values are couched in distinctly psychological if not psychoanalytic terms. The central value appears as "affection," broadly defined as congeniality and the absence of hostility. Democracy is construed as the social manifestation of the "democratic personality" produced by the manipulatory processes. This "democratic personality" has been described as "perfectly socialized, perfectly free of inhibitions and anxiety, perfectly content, perfectly peaceful" by Robert Horwitz, a leading critic of Lasswell. The reign of elitism, then, in Lasswell's vision, is replaced by a radical egalitarianism, based upon the ubiquity of human personality and its malleability.

JOHN DEWEY

The theories of the democratic elitists are countered by a vigorous defense of pluralism. The democratic viewpoint of John Dewey is an integral adjunct of the pluralism that follows from the assertion that no objective judgmental standard can be thought to exist, save subjective conceptions of self-interest. This subjective utilitarianism implies the "open society," the primacy of individual desire, the comprehensive rejection of authoritative values or formulae, as against immediate perceptions of well-being. This pluralistic individualism, the off-spring of pragmatism, is tempered, in Dewey's case, by two important considerations: (1) the scientific viability of measurement, so as to make judgment possible regarding the efficacy of means and (2) the need to establish some conception of a social consensus upon which pluralistic diversity can rest and be preserved. These are, in reality, quite different considerations, yet they do conjoin to the extent that they imply social control. Such control exists in the form of a device for the creation of reasonable alternatives, this reasonableness being defined as some reliable expectation as to consequences. Alternative courses of action, in terms of effects on practical human life, therefore, can be articulated through the operation of empirical science. The heart of democracy, then, for Dewey, was a state of affairs in which: (1) human choice was primary, yet (2) those choices were presumably predicated upon the articulation of reasonable alternatives or guides to consequences.

To a large extent, Dewey's hypothesis regarding democracy turns on a moral precept: the resolution of the "moral question" depends on an empirically-possible examination of the effects of action. Conversely, the antithesis of democracy was the enshrinement of moral abstractions and static mythologies that both constricted the progressive explorations of human intelligence and denied the primacy of immediate human concerns.

In more directly political terms, Dewey dealt with the problem of the necessary social consensus that would underpin the democratic society. That consensus, in non-institutional terms, meant a universal recognition of the moral axiom expressed above. Its core premise was the awareness of the indispensability of human development, a view of such development similar to that of J. S. Mill that emphasized the growth of the human personality through reflection upon experience. From this developmental concept sprang Dewey's defense of freedom, equality, and social progress. All procedural and institutional considerations must, then, obey the injunction of self-development. Dewey once wrote, "Democratic political forms are simply the best means that human wit has devised up to a special time in history." Participation, then, is defended on two grounds: (1) it is vital, given Dewey's theory, to the process of policy selection since the consensus or majority alone can form a proper base for social judgment and (2) the act of participation, by itself, is essential to self-development.

A prominent feature of Dewey's concept of democracy was a virtual "faith" in the expanding capabilities of human beings, in sum, the potentialities of intelligence were only partially developed.

Freudian or neo-positivistic reservations about such competency failed to deter him. Education—of the type advocated by Dewey himself—was the key to the expansion of the democratic vista. Such an education would, in effect, strengthen rather than dilute the egalitarian thrust of democracy, an egalitarianism that, in Dewey's terms, was defined as an equal opportunity for self-development.

Freedom, for Dewey, was not wholly egocentric—he explicitly rejects Mill's extreme individualism. He distinguishes between "freedom of action" as possibly anti-social and the "freedom of the intelligence," which he presupposes will permit the growth of intelligence, which will stimulate social compatibility and even congeniality. Dewey envisions a distinct socializing motif in the operation of intelligence, assuming that the blend of individual volition and intelligence will produce "socialization" rather than Hobbesian conflict.

These viewpoints became almost synonymous with what the twentieth century came to call "popular democracy." Dewey's thought bridges the liberalism of the last century with the more collectivistic or socialized trends of the twentieth by casting "self-development" in a social context, by preserving pluralism by wedding it to a problematic, progressivistic orientation, by broadening ideas of equality to embrace social participation in addition to legal and political guarantees, by resting the value component of democracy on a psychological foundation.

JOSEPH TUSSMAN

Joseph Tussman, a contemporary democratic theorist, belongs within the inherited frame of pragmatism. In his *Obligation and the Body Politic*, published in 1960, Tussman observes:

> If I had to select a figure of speech which, upon analysis, would reveal the basic dilemma of our political life, I would choose the "marketplace of ideas." "The best test of truth," one of our sages has told us, "is the power of the thought to get itself accepted in the competition of the market!" How I wish some genius had thrown equal light on another dark area of our lives by proclaiming that the

best test of virtue is "the power of a desire to get itself accepted in
the competition of the market." (p. 104)

The "sage" referred to, by Tussman, is William James and
James's pragmatic spirit courses through Tussman's ideas. His cardinal hypothesis is a reaffirmation of the potentialities of the mass
electorate, but, Tussman adds, it must develop into "a genuinely
deliberative tribunal, capable of dealing responsibly with fundamental issues." Like Dewey, he sees education as the primary means,
allied with a transformation of the citizenry into a more politicalized
awareness. This awareness involves abandoning notions about government as simply an expression of transient wants. Also, government cannot rest upon a "balancing" of interests or even proceed
on the basis of facile compromise. These illusions, Tussman argues,
are the result of a "bargaining spirit," an over-emphasis on competition, an erroneous parallel between government and the "market."

The problem, at base, he contends, arises from a confusion
between the citizen's recognition of his "public" and "private"
roles. In the former, the citizenry need to form differing conceptions of propriety and judgment that are basically different from
egocentric individualism and "marketplace democracy." The citizen
must accept the full implications of the tribunate—Tussman takes
very seriously the idea of the electorate as the "Fourth Branch of
Government."

Tussman's observations are not strikingly original, but they do
present us with a depiction of democracy that retains pluralism
while moving far from the tenets of classical liberalism. In addition,
he counters democratic elitism with a sweeping conceptualization of
participation or, as it is sometimes called, "participatory democracy."
His reaction to the embattled state of contemporary democracy is to
revive, in concrete terms, the idea of "popular sovereignty."

PETER BACHRACH

Peter Bachrach has not only met the arguments of the elitists
head-on in his *The Theory of Democratic Elitism,* but also has

advanced a pluralistically-construed argument on behalf of "participatory democracy." Bachrach's own theory of democracy follows from his initial observation that

> By conceiving of man's political interest solely in terms of that which accrues to him from government, the democratic elitist implicitly rejects the contention of classical theorists that interests also include the opportunity for development which accrues from participation in meaningful political decisions. (p. 95)

Bachrach wishes to reaffirm the "classical" by insisting upon participation as necessary to self-development, this latter condition being the foundation upon which the free society depends. But how, Bachrach asks, can this "classical" concept, ethical in essence, be reconciled with the requirements of the present?

Bachrach's answer, in brief, is, first, to reject the temptation to assume that society is unalterably shaped by "illiberal and impersonal forces" and to proceed, instead, from unabashedly normative theses, the primary among them being the "self-development of the individual." A theory of democracy, hence, ought to be built upon the proposition that "the majority of individuals stand to gain in self-esteem and growth toward a fuller affirmation of their potentialities by participating more actively in meaningful community decisions." In order to accomplish this end, Bachrach is willing to "politicalize" many aspects of heretofore private life. He defends this idea by asserting that the forms of political education that would result from wider-ranging participation would not only qualitatively enhance the individual, but would also benefit the quality of private life, e.g., the internal operations of factories, offices, commercial corporations, and other private endeavors. It is clear that the broadening of participation in these areas would require not only a governmental initiative, but also the acquiescence to the notion that the internal operations of such social institutions are predominantly political in nature. Bachrach would anticipate a wholesome improvement of the capacities of the citizenry, thus allaying the fear of elitists regarding the masses' anti-democratic proclivities.

HENRY KARIEL

To place Henry Kariel among the pluralists may seem an odd decision in view of the fact that he has been highly critical of pluralism
(i.e., *The Decline of American Pluralism*). But what Kariel complains of regarding pluralism is the tendency to make it an end in
itself, to the exclusion of the progressive enhancement of democratic
values. Thus, within another context, Kariel is a "substantialist" in
democratic thought, a believer in the existence of substantive democratic principles, as against the "proceduralists," who view democracy solely as a set of arrangements. This substantialist approach,
strongly stressing "participation"—widening the range of popular
involvement—causes Kariel to reject the import of democratic elitism, much like Peter Bachrach, who also encourages a broadening of
participation. One cannot call the elitists advocates of pluralism, although they seem to endorse a circulation of elites or polyarchies in
contrast to an espousal of specific values. Pluralism implies the vital
toleration of diversified shades of opinion and interest, not the competition for what must be, finally, authoritative allocations of values
and influence. Democratic pluralism has always presupposed a foundational adherence to certain liberal precepts which, although some
democratic elitists declare their admiration, cannot be presumed to
prevail, *prima facie,* under the assumption of the elitist imperative.
It is for these reasons, then, that writers such as Kariel and Bachrach, often critical of pluralism in explicit application, belong to
this orientation (within our particular schema) in contrast to the
category of democratic elitism. It may well be reasonable, on the
other hand, to separate more or less traditional pluralists from
"participationists."

Kariel's principal concern in the area of democratic theory is
the need to create a psychological climate in which there could be a
more or less spontaneous motivation toward change and improvement. He assumes that the democratization of social practice and
arrangement will result in greater aptitudes for and acceptance of
change and an enlarged productivity. The integration of individual
and social desires will result, he contends, from this widespread
participatory effort. "Democracy," he comments, "will grow natu-

rally from the interpersonal relations experienced in tolerant and generous community living."

Kariel's thoughts on democracy and pluralism obviously go far beyond this very cursory account, but the general nature of his position is instructive, affording a striking contrast with the power emphasis of elite theorists. Yet the "values" admired by Kariel and other "participationists" are markedly similar to the "democratic personality" envisioned by Lasswell. Beyond the position taken by Dewey, the pluralists have appeared to move more decidedly toward the thesis that pluralism is not really an end in itself, but a condition conducive to the stimulation of psycho-sociological attitudes and behavioral characteristics presumed to be "democratic." From Tussman onward, democratic pluralism has sought to disengage democratic theory from an entrepreneurial orientation, to move from the idea of an equality of opportunity to a concept of an equality of condition. Tussman sought to separate the spheres of participation and their prevailing protocols into public activity and private endeavor. But Bachrach and Kariel are more socially monistic and less pragmatic; the later pluralists see participation as leading to more or less specific social results, the primary characteristic of which would be more comprehensive egalitarianism and a social conformity based upon rather fixed conceptions of "personality development."

CHRISTIAN BAY AND KENNETH MEGILL

There is a still more radical orientation in contemporary democratic thought, illustrated by the writings of Christian Bay and Kenneth Megill, both of whom enjoy a certain identification with the "new radicalism" to be discussed in chapter nine. Both Bay and Megill suggest, in the manner of Bernard Shaw's oft-quoted remark about Christianity, that the only thing wrong with democracy is that it has never been tried.

Bay is highly critical of much conventional democratic theory, which he argues is really not value-free or objective, but is, in fact, "conservative" and "anti-political." This democratic theory, in Bay's view, fails to address itself to human needs and values. Politics, he contends, is not merely the study of power, but must also include human welfare and the public good.

Bay's position seems very much akin to the pluralists, since he posits individual human freedom as the elemental political goal and this freedom is conceived of in social and psychological terms. This realization of freedom will demand, for Bay, a willingness to boldly measure social practice against the norm of freedom and to demolish any and all existing conditions detrimental to this end, embracing what Bay terms a "priority" for those "individuals who are most severely oppressed" and "the least likely to achieve redress by way of the ordinary democratic processes."

Bay's reflections on human development include the observation that rational political participation is strongly hampered by anxiety. Such anxieties force individuals into political choices dictated by presumably neurotic motivations and predispose them toward conventional and generally accepted viewpoints. In his article "Politics and Pseudopolitics" (1965), Bay argues that "the development of strictly political incentives in the individual, then, depends on a gradual process of liberation from a preoccupation with personal anxieties and worries." We must confront, says Bay, "the fact that most of our citizens live too harassed lives or lack the education or opportunities for reflection to permit them the real satisfactions and full dignity of democratic citizenship."

The supposition must be, then, in Bay's opinion, that a radical social reconstruction—to eliminate these handicaps—must precede a participatory democracy that would permit those conditions leading to "real satisfactions and full dignity of democratic citizenship." On what basis could such an enterprise take place? Bay's response is to call for a new form of socio-political research in order to provide the social norms for such a liberated society (about which, by the way, Bay is not particularly explicit). The argument is reminiscent of Kariel's, but appears more radical in its willingness to coercively eliminate the social obstacles to a conception of self-realization that lies under the aegis of a presumably authoritative new political sociology.

Kenneth Megill's outlook, contained in his *The New Democratic Theory*, is an attempt to restate democratic theory in terms of a modified Marxism and to project it within the momentum of cultural revolution. Megill is quite precise: "The primary question of contemporary democratic theory is, in the end, the question of the proper organization of the revolutionary movement."

Megill rejects "liberal democracy" principally because he sees it to be the political ideology of a more rudimentary and repugnant social phenomenon: free-enterprise capitalism. Under the obvious influence of the contemporary Marxist, Georg Lukas, Megill calls for a "radicalization" of the political perspective that would create a new neo-Marxist synthesis. This "radicalization" would have popular democracy emerge as a result of the political triumph of a coalition of the oppressed, to include the "culturally deprived" middle classes. Megill sees a new democratic culture arising from new forms of socialization, eliminating the individual-society dichotomy.

Social alienation is to be overcome. "A political movement which aims at fundamental social change is possible today because a large number of people experience a deep and profound sense of alienation from the political and social order," concludes Megill. Alienation is to be abolished by giving workers greater control over productive processes, over the "working situation," and by the subjugation of the bureaucracy.

Democracy—in Megill's conception of it as being the destruction of the oppressive conditions of a free market economy—means the creation of a new-found freedom "based upon communities organized around the real life of man." The model for the "real life of man," for Megill, is provided by "the life of man as a working being." Democracy, hence, for Megill, is simply "a way of living," a synonym for a type of communalization based upon a control of working and living conditions.

Such an objective not only requires a revolution, asserts Megill, but also the revolutionary *élan* itself constitutes the basis of the new society. In somewhat polemical style, in *The New Democratic Theory,* Megill sums up:

> A new era of history has begun, and a new movement to radically change the world is a reality. The new democratic theory is an articulation of this force. The theory is only beginning to be worked out,

but it is already a reality. Hope for a genuine democratic social order depends upon the success of the movement now being built. (pp. 163–64)

DEMOCRACY AT THE CROSSROADS

Democracy has stood, nervously, at the crossroads throughout much of the twentieth century. It has been assaulted by the mass radicalisms of the century, fascism and communism; it has been harshly criticized by the conservative anti-democrats; it has been virtually defined out of existence by a newer social radicalism. But democracy has also suffered from a growing fragmentization of its defense, as is illustrated, of course, by the schism between pluralists and elitists.

The principal difficulty in constructing contemporary democratic theory lies in discovering a viable philosophical base. Such a base did exist in the individualistic democratic theory of the nineteenth century and, substantially, for the pragmatic popular democracy of the first half of this century. But, presently, both elitism and pluralism, as theoretical outlooks, suffer from certain philosophical uncertainties. Elitism's primary problem grows out of the difficulty of conceiving the "circulation of elites" in wholly operational or mechanistic terms. The implication—in Dahl and Sartori, for example—that elite competition can take place entirely under the umbrella of democratic procedural protocols is simplistic. Elitism, even as conceived by democratic theorists, invariably invites a mood of dogmatism, of rival claims to authority couched in absolutist terminologies. The postulation of "polyarchies" does not meet the demand for reasonable discourse about social ends, it does not adequately insure the shape of social arrangements, it does not directly face the undeniable cultural anxieties that have been well-documented by social critics, *unless* some qualitative standard, philosophically derived, can be formulated by which the competing claims of elites can be judged. And even if that objection can be met, the question can be fairly asked if, in fact, such a normative mode of discrimination between elites can be accurately viewed as reconcilable with *democratic* theory.

Moreover, the Lasswellian argument for elitism as a transition to an egalitarian utopia, a metamorphosis from a closed society to an open one, is dubious. It is dubious not only in terms of relinquishing, ultimately, social control, but also in terms of the validity of talking seriously about a "democratic personality," innate or induced. Putatively empirical discussion of so-called "democratic" and "authoritarian" personalities has been singularly unsatisfying. In the democratic context, it is difficult to reconcile such a doctrinaire view of human nature and attitudes with the presumably heterodox character of democratic values.

The pluralists face the elementary dilemma of attempting to shift their argument from an endorsement of equality of opportunity to a defense of an equality of condition without jettisoning pluralism altogether. If pluralism is now thought to be a "means" rather than an "end," what real defense is there, finally, for the maintenance of the pluralistic society? Too much of pluralist argument rests upon the shifting sands of psychological speculation, much of it as manipulatory in implication as the views of their erstwhile adversaries, the elitists. The supposition that a widened "participation" invariably enhances "self-development" and that this, in turn, creates social progress and harmony is an interesting (but not altogether original) theory, but it lacks anything approaching a solid empirical validation. Both Bachrach and Kariel display a vast faith in the hypotheses of certain social psychologists regarding the results of voluntary participation in producing a salutory consensus and motivation toward the social good. Kariel, for instance, enthusiastically cites the experiments of Kurt Lewin, among which was one in which a body of students were better led to eat whole-wheat bread by "voluntary group decision" than by being lectured to and by means of private, subjective evaluations of their choice. Such an implicit analogy is simply picturesque—the assumption that people deciding the life-and-death issues pertinent to the political would behave similarly is questionable.

Christian Bay's call for a new research orientation that would supply a normative basis for social reconstruction from which a renewed democratic polity would emerge suffers from causal difficulties. If this research is to proceed from axiological assumptions, it is doubtful that it could yield scientific maxims of such a non-contentious nature that one could feel justified in wholesale social rearrangement on their authority. One detects a covert moral absolutism. If this research undertaking, on the other hand, were to be valuationally "neutral," it would be hard to (1) sustain the assumption that judgments on profoundly significant social values could be derived from a purely scientific conceptualization; and (2) on what basis would one judge between competing scientific conceptualizations, unless one held some criterion of social good?

The presence of psychological anxieties and the methods by which they are supposed to be resolved have an effect upon the political climate. But on what basis can we predict the more or less specific political repercussions or attitudes that follow from a reduction of anxiety or, for that matter, any other form of social neurosis? Moreover, what we know about neurosis suggests that human psychical aberration is unlike physical disease; we do not "cure" or "resolve" neurosis, we only reduce its impairments on function. The possible homeostasis Bay suggests, however "democratic" in terms of self-development, may well be productive of new and unforeseen maladjustments and tensions that require on-going forms of social therapy. In sum, the conviction that the more "democratic" an individual or society is the more "healthy" he or it is requires a more formidable justification than is now available in democratic literature.

It is with these and other dilemmas that contemporary democratic thought must wrestle. These perplexities need not, however, obscure the over-riding concern of democracy: how to preserve and enhance an ancient regard for the importance and dignity of the human individual in the face of pressures, changes and dehumanizing temptations, all intensely active in the twentieth century world. The philosophical discomfitures afflicting contemporary democratic thought—and they are considerable—need not diminish the awesome responsibility borne by defenders of democracy. Democracy does not enjoy a monopoly of concern for preserving the motifs of human freedom and the expression of spiritual values, but it remains, currently, the principal inheritor of the classical humanisms and the ethical precepts of the Judeo–Christian heritage.

FOR ADDITIONAL READING

Bachrach, Peter, *The Theory of Democratic Elitism*. Boston: Little, Brown, 1967.

BAY, CHRISTIAN, *The Structure of Freedom*. Stanford, Calif.: Stanford University Press, 1958.

DAHL, ROBERT, *A Preface to Democratic Theory*. Chicago: University of Chicago Press, 1956.

DEWEY, JOHN, *The Public and Its Problems*. New York: Henry Holt & Co., 1927.

HOOK, SIDNEY, *Reason, Social Myths and Democracy*. New York: Harper, 1966 (orig. pub. 1940).

KARIEL, HENRY, *The Decline of American Pluralism*. Stanford, Calif.: Stanford University Press, 1961.

LASSWELL, HAROLD, *The Political Writings of Harold D. Lasswell*. New York: Free Press, 1951.

MEGILL, K. A., *The New Democratic Theory*. New York: Free Press, 1970.

PARETO, VILFREDO, *Sociological Writings* (trans. by D. Mirfin). New York: Praeger, 1966.

SARTORI, GIOVANNI, *Democratic Theory*. New York: Prager, 1965 (orig. pub. 1958).

SCHUMPETER, J. A., *Capitalism, Socialism and Democracy*. New York: Harper, 1950 (orig. pub. 1942).

TUSSMANN, JOSEPH, *Obligation and the Body Politic*. New York: Oxford University Press, 1960.

SEVEN

The Recoil of
Taste

Conservatism

At the beginning of the nineteenth century, two primary forces were in collision: the traditions of the *ancien regime,* the old order, and the new social forces unleashed by the ideas underlying the French Revolution and, later, the subsequent philosophies underlying an equally critical revolution, the industrial one. The spasms of the French Revolution died down for a time, resurfacing here and there, for example, the unrest of 1848, the appearance of radical socialism, the advent of Marxism and, by the end of that century, the political prominence of mass tastes.

But for most of the last century, the principal social and intellectual struggle took place between the old order, endeavoring to maintain itself, and the newer movements spawned by the enormous cultural changes wrought by the Industrial Revolution. The outcome was inevitable; the old order gave way or, more properly, retreated from political control into intellectual and ideological criticism. Save for an occasional upsurge of political vitality, like Disraeli's "Tory Democracy," the political and social perspectives of the old aristocracy succumbed to the new wave of the middle classes and political liberalism was the doctrine of the day.

But a wide variety of political thinkers found themselves in opposition to these triumphant trends, recoiling from the full import of the Industrial Revolution. While inheriting the eighteenth century traditions of Edmund Burke and John Adams, the nineteenth century opposition to liberalism took many forms, political and literary. In America, the opposition was provided by such men as Hawthorne, Calhoun, Brownson, Melville, and Henry Adams. In Britain, liberalism came under attack from such personages as Coleridge, Disraeli, and Carlyle. In France, the opposition included de Maistre, Bonald, Toqueville and Taine; in Germany, Goethe and von Savigny provided the opposition.

By the turn of the nineteenth century, the political prospects of what was now being called "conservatism" were dim, indeed. The focus of political controversy was upon contending aspects of liberalism and the emergence of social radicalism. The full shape of the Industrial Revolution had now emerged. The twentieth century was to be an era dominated by technology and social democracy.

Since the waning years of the nineteenth century, political conservatism had largely assumed a literary mode of expression. In fact, it was more an intellectual conservatism than an overtly political one. However, the grimmer aspects of the Industrial Revolution and the prospect of a more violent struggle between the reigning liberal-oriented political elites and the revolutionary-inclined tribunes of the masses intensified conservative social criticism.

THE NEW HUMANISTS

Early in the century, in the United States, this social conservatism was to find an expression among a group of Harvard University academics, the "New Humanists," led by Irving Babbitt, Paul Elmer More, and George Santayana. Babbitt, a professor of literature, was alarmed over what he estimated were the literary and social excesses of Romanticism (especially its arch-personification, Rousseau) and argued for a revival of classicism, which included a regard for moral standards, social hierarchy, and ethical pre-eminence as the basis for political and social leadership. He was extremely critical of the lack of discipline in popular democracy, along with its emotionalism and what he concluded was its inherent preference for mediocrity.

Paul Elmer More, only briefly an academician, was at base a Christian neo-Platonist, strongly imbued with the Greek ideal of aristocracy, the personal cultivation of moral rectitude and talent, and the necessary differentiations in human worth, as against radical egalitarianism. George Santayana, a major American philosopher and leader of a philosophical movement known as *critical realism,* was equally convinced that mass democracy was suffocating all talent and excellence, and he made a particularly strong argument for the idea of a natural social hierarchy and an inescapable inequality among men.

These men, different in many respects, were allied in their detestation of the emerging mass culture with its technological base and its disregard of civilized tradition and, especially, its almost deliberate ugliness. The influence of the New Humanists was not inconsequential. Among Babbitt's students was Thomas Stearnes Eliot, the poet, who became a major voice of social conservatism. His viewpoint blended the social criticism and ethical temper of Babbitt with a defense of the irreplacability of Christian orthodoxy. However Babbitt, Santayana, More, and Eliot might disagree regarding theology, all were committed to a humanistic revival, choosing to define *humanism* in its original meaning: the inculcation of moral standards by the study of classical literature.

OTHER CONSERVATIVES

Such misgivings about the drift of the culture were not confined to the United States. In Spain José Ortega y Gasset appeared, whose first work, *Meditations on Quixote,* was published in 1911. Ortega, combining a traditional Spanish conservatism with the influences of his German education, particularly the philosophies of Nietzsche, Husserl (Swiss), and the Marburg Realists, wrote of the destruction of man's cultural identifications and of a deepening alienation from his roots, due in large measure to the victory of popular ideology and the purveyance of egalitarian myths. His *The Revolt of the Masses* describes this predicament.

Elsewhere in Europe intellectual conservatism was stirring. In Britain, neo-idealism was extant earlier in the century; its last and most formidable advocate, F. H. Bradley, died in 1924. America, too, had a neo-idealist tradition, in the hands of Josiah Royce and William Hocking. In Britain, ethical realism persisted despite the rise of positivistic ethics. G. E. Moore is the prime example, along with the British process philosophers, Whitehead and Alexander. English historicism also produced two politically conservative thinkers: R. G. Collingwood and Michael Oakeshott.

On the continent, neo-realism grew stronger; Max Scheler and Nicolai Hartmann are the most celebrated examples. Their ethics were highly suggestive of conservative social viewpoints.

Theological argument, too, reinforced conservatism. Protestant neo-orthodoxy was ranged against "modernism" and emphasized human sinful proclivities and attacked the optimism and "social gospelism" of the times. The prominent figures were Karl Barth, Paul Tillich, and Reinhold Niebuhr. Catholics, as well, reacted against social radicalism, both clergy and laymen, such as Father John Courtney Murray and Ralph Adams Cram, the architect.

One somewhat curious side of the conservative current was a school of American anthropologists who generally supported the thesis of Nordic superiority and eugenic disaster as a result of mass wars and excessive social egalitarianism. The most important of these was Madison Grant, the author of *The Passing of the Great Race,* whose influence is still to be evidenced in the contemporary works of Stephen Possony and Nathaniel Weyl.

T. S. ELIOT: SPOKESMAN FOR
CONSERVATISM

Perhaps no one better captured the mood of the social and intellectual conservatives in the years between the wars than T. S. Eliot. Eliot's well-known poem, *The Waste Land,* published in 1922, expressed the conservative's anguish over the demolition of tradition and the moral and aesthetic sterility of twentieth century life. Eliot's poetry, verse plays, and essays, especially *The Idea of the Christian Community* and *Notes Toward a Definition of Culture,* did more than express his "classicism," "royalism," and Anglo-Catholicism. They darkly suggested the advent of a new barbarism unless certain elements of Western culture were restored: the dominance of Judeo-Christian ethics as a social base and the recognition of the aristocratic principle, i.e., the legitimacy of social claims based upon self-cultivation.

Eliot and the pre-World War II conservatives joined in three main outlooks: (1) the necessity for social well-being to rest upon traditional values and an aristocratic perspective to counter the egalitarianism and vulgarity of the prevailing ethos; (2) the need to reemphasize duty and social loyalty; and (3) to assert the primacy of the community over the egocentric individual.

In sum, these pre-World War II conservatives were disposed to criticize popular democracy on moral grounds and to espouse distinctly aristocratic ideas, but their major source of disquiet was the havoc, the injury to social order, they thought they could trace to the philistinism of the Industrial Revolution.

THE NEW CONSERVATISM

After the bloody interregnum of World War II, the term *conservatism* came into somewhat more common usage as a result of the appearance of the New Conservatism of the 1950s. To some extent, this more recent activity arose from a somewhat belated attention to the works of Edmund Burke, dubbed by some as the "father of modern conservatism." Also contributing was a mounting anxiety regarding the rapidity of social change and the ramifications of widespread moral relativism and even ethical nihilism.

This era saw the appearance of the works of Peter Viereck, Richard Weaver, and Russell Kirk. Kirk, particularly, commencing with his *The Conservative Mind* in 1953, contributed to fusing intellectual elements having a common disposition toward historical conservatism. This was the beginning of what more lately has been called traditionalism. This mood was also mirrored abroad in the works of Bertrand de Jouvenel, the French political philosopher, and Eric Voegelin. Voegelin's work, much of which was written in the United States, has culminated in a multi-volume effort, *Order and History*.

The New Conservatism gained some momentum. Among the early figures in this movement were Francis Graham Wilson, Will Herberg, Leo Strauss, Thomas Molnar, and Eliseo Vivas. Although the shade of Edmund Burke hung over this assemblage, it was also apparent that this American intellectual movement also returned to the tap-roots of classical federalism, the political philosophy of Adams, Fisher Ames, and Chancellor Kent. Indeed, there was evident a certain tension between traditionalists of an aristocratic, cosmopolitan posture and those primarily identifying with the "American tradition"—as certain conservative-learning historians, such as Clinton Rossiter and Daniel Boorstin, pointed out.

As a matter of fact, the New Conversatism showed some signs, by the early 1960s, of fragmenting, due, in part, to its enhanced popular respectability and due to the fact that "conservatism," as a piece of terminology, had become a part of the American political vocabulary—Barry Goldwater ran for the Presidency in 1964 under this informal label. The increasing popularity of the term led to wide differences of view regarding its meaning. Recognizable were at least four main sub-groupings: (1) traditional historical conservatives, largely Burkeans or neo-Aristotelians, aristocratic, cosmopolitan, anti-democratic, and principally concerned with ethical restoration; (2) American conservative traditionalists who wished to rest their case on the uniqueness and majesty of the continuities of American classical federalism and republicanism; (3) those who denied the feasibility of democracy by means of the "iron law of oligarchy" argument and, therefore, advocated some form of social elitism; (4) those who favored a "libertarian" point of view, interpreting conservatism to mean a revival of nineteenth century individualism and governmental laissez-faire.

These groups were not entirely exclusive of one another in some instances and some conservatives argued in favor of "fusionism," a connecting of one or more of these orientations. Yet it would be impossible to reconcile all, if not most, of these differing attitudes and thereby the considerable confusion regarding the meaning of "conservatism" in the twentieth century is produced.

If one attempted, in the broadest manner, to link the historical development of conservative thought (at least since Burke) to its present configurations, perhaps the lowest common demoninators might be these: (1) a defense of ethical absolutism; (2) a rejection of meliorism and a cautious attitude toward social change; (3) a mood of political realism; (4) a denial of a comprehensive view of human equality and a belief in a natural hierarchy; (5) a regard for the importance of the social continuity; (6) a denial of the idea that politics is the highest concern of man; (7) an admiration for agrarian values.

Furthermore,

1. Twentieth century conservatives have invariably supported the objectivity and immutability of value. Their position has been a resolute defense of a reasonably wide-based interpretation of ethical realism. They have differed as to the source and nature of this objective ethical mandate. Many, like Eliot or, more recently, Kirk, have asserted the necessity of theism—conviction of the existence of a Supreme Being—as a basis for the conservative espousal of a moral order, while others like Babbitt and Vivas have offered non-theistic explanations for the objectivity and authority of moral values.

   To the conservative, value relativism is anathema. Not only are values independent of human will, but they are binding, in one way or another, and most contemporary conservatives believe that the natural order, societies, and other communal organisms are themselves actualizations of the moral order or that they contain an ethical component. Freedom, hence, can never be a freedom *from* moral injunction, even if the will is free to perversely reject the moral obligation. This concept, as we will see later, constitutes the major aspect of conservatism's critique of popular democracy.

   The conservative uses a variety of means to justify his view of the viability of an objective moral order: he may appeal to logical necessity, to religious revelation, to intuition, to irrational or instinctual awareness, to "social memory," to historical analysis, or to the phenomenon of the private conscience, but the crux of his social theory rests upon his ability to satisfactorily demonstrate the presence and constancy of moral value. Such a conviction brings with it a judgmental potentiality: societies, governments and individual men can be appraised in accordance with this unvarying ethical standard. It makes possible, for the conservative, serious discussion about "right" and "wrong" that does not depend upon opinion or poll-taking. Possession of moral insight, if it can be demonstrated, brings with it authority, the authority of knowledge over ignorance. It makes possible, too, a conservative concept of legitimate leadership based upon ethical attainments.

2. Meliorism is a term used to describe the belief in the inevitability of progress. The conservative rejects the idea that human history is the record of inexorable improvement and this stance causes him to be more skeptical of change than others more essentially optimistic in outlook. The conservative insistence upon prudence in advocating innovation, although springing from an unwillingness to assume that change is, ipso facto, improvement, is rooted even more fundamentally in the belief that while progress is not inevitable, human nature is basically unchanging and that this human nature, being highly resistant to wholesale improvement, can cause jeopardies to the continuity of civilization. The conservative viewpoint insists that man's nature is savage and recalcitrant if not constrained by moral rectitude. This being the case, the human experience is a highly variable record of achievement, alternatively splendid or sordid.

   Change is to be approached cautiously, the conservative argues, not only because progress is inconstant and human nature fixed, but also because the benefits currently enjoyed always far exceed those things requiring reform. Thus, change must be, in every case, miniscule in proportion to that which is preserved, and radical and drastic change endangers, by its sheer scope, the advantages currently to be utilized.

   Also, the conservative entertains the suspicion that often change may be undertaken for its own sake—innovation being prompted only by a restless appetite for social excitement. Such a motivation is suggestive of a dangerous immaturity that needs to be tempered by more sober and disciplined minds, asserts the conservative.

3. The view of human nature held by most conservatives when allied with their historicism is a type of political realism and makes prudence the premier political virtue. Conservatism, by and large, eschews the doctrinaire, the idealization of social planning and social abstractions in general, in favor of a more limited and presumably more flexible political response. Conservatism appears disdainful of formulae and dubious about the effectiveness of positive law in many areas of social relationships. There is in conservatism a rather skeptical tenor of mind that, if it does not manifest itself in religious and ethical matters, does pervade its explicitly political attitudes. It claims to be "humanistic" without being "humanitarianistic" and by that distinction to suggest a preference for more intimate benevolences than a dedication to as spacious an abstraction as "humanity."

   In many conservative writers, Eliot and Ortega, for example, one senses this political realism in the form of a vivid awareness of the close proximity of any culture to a barbaric regression. This motif always, in conservatism, reinforces a firm belief in social control, even a social control that may be, in crisis periods, quite severe. Peter Viereck, himself not a militant theist by any means, once defended organized religion on the ground that it helped "pull the claws of the Noble Savage" —a thesis strangely reminiscent (except in its import) of Marx's famous dictum regarding religion as the "opiate of the people." Candidly speaking, the viewpoint of conservatives concerning the capabilities of the "masses" is not flattering; for the conservatives there are few "mute and inglorious Miltons." Without beneficial and even paternalistic guidance, the vast proportion of men would likely succumb to the temptations of intemperate passion and atavistic appetite. Such is the genesis of conservatism's political realism.

4. Views regarding human equality vary among the conservatives. The religionists among them would, for illustration, grant an equality of all men before God—a viewpoint almost universally held in the thirteenth century. Few conservatives would question the desirability of legal equality. Some would support a certain measure of political equality. But, on balance, the conservatives are distinctly anti-egalitarian as regards social equality and they take up this position on the basis of two convictions: (1) they would deny that men are intrinsically equal and (2) they would reject the desirability of procedural equality.

In somewhat more detail, the general anti-egalitarian attitude of twentieth century conservatism involves these premises: (1) a society is a natural hierarchy; (2) it is irrational and unjustifiable, on the evidence, to suppose men to be equal in terms of capacities; (3) a social division of labor exists that demands that individual men enjoy differing prerogatives due to the differences in their social vocations, qualitative differences in their discharge of duties, and degree of ethical self-discipline.

The hierarchical character of society—from which inequalities of station proceed—are thought to be *natural,* that is, the stratified society is an unavoidable configuration determined by the natural origins of society. Social organicists, in the main, the conservatives, dismiss the idea of society as a human artifact, decisively amenable to human will. All societies are, for the conservative, "pecking orders," in a manner of speaking, although it is possible to corrupt the natural hierarchy and substitute one produced as a human contrivance. To be fair, the contemporary conservatives are certainly not admirers of repressive autocracy and display an overwhelming aversion for tyranny. Their argument is that repressive autocracy arises in two prominent forms: the "rule of the mob" or those despots propelled into power by the collapse of a well-ordered and humane social hierarchy.

This natural hierarchy is expressed in terms of differences between individual men, but most conservatives also feel the need to conceive the hierarchical society in terms of social classes. Conservatives in the Burkean tradition look upon social classes as loose confederations of like-conditioned individuals of roughly comparable capacities. These social classes are desirable, contends the conservative, in that they both structure the society and yet remain "open" to membership on the basis of talent or merit. The apex of the stratification of social classes is, for many conservatives, a "natural aristocracy" or as one English writer put it, a "meritocracy." Classes are useful, asserts the conservative, but membership in them does not imply any categorical superiority, only a differing set of social obligations and responsibilities and, doubtless, a recognizable difference in the styles of life.

A few conservatives—but not many—look at the class hierarchy in more concrete ethnic terms, harkening back to Madison Grant or Henry Fairfield Osborne. Their primary interest appears to be the relationship between levels of intelligence and ethnic origins. The issue of genetic factors in the capacities of racial groups is still being scientifically contested, but most conservatives do not suggest any qualitative differential on an ethnic basis that is pertinent to the idea of the social hierarchy. Instead, they tend to stress the internal integrity of "class"—values, ethnic and otherwise—as a part of their objection to social leveling.

It is not really the *idea* of human equality that the conservatives reject; it is the concept of the *enforcement* of equality in a social context that, in their view, denies the natural and desirable diversities between people. To enforce equality, they argue, must ultimately lead to the enforcement not only of equality among people, but equality among codes of behavior, human creativity, and expectation. The danger in social leveling is the introduction of a debilitating mediocrity and, at worst, a moral stagnation and a critical loss of freedom and creative motivation.

Social leveling, say the conservatives, denies to men their just due, earned by the superior performance of duty and by the excellence of their industry and accomplishments. Human benevolence, they assert, cannot mean the abandonment of a discrimination between the deserving and the undeserving. The "welfare state" is an introduction to a social order shorn of necessary and legitimate reward, a state of affairs in which indolence, viciousness, and irresponsibility will receive equal treatment with talent, industriousness, self-control, and service. The conservatives attribute these regrettable trends to an over-emphasis on an equality of "rights" and a disregard for collateral "duties." "Rights," to the conservative, follow from the adequate discharge of duties and they do not exist *in vacuo*.

Moreover, they consider the enthusiasm for social leveling—the omnibus enforcement of equality—as a cynical stratagem of popular politicians who, with only partially hidden elitist aspirations, pander to the mass vanities by flattering, if unsustainable, proclamations of equality. This is finally socially injurious, because such conceptions of equality are artificial, and even governmental enforcement cannot maintain them against the awareness of persistent inequalities.

The social Darwinist, against whom traditional conservatives vigorously dissent, had long endorsed an "equality of opportunity," since the elemental thesis of social Darwinism was the right of every man to anything he could get. The conservative opposes the enforcement of an "equality of opportunity" on two counts: (1) men ought not to be persuaded to seek that which is unquestionably beyond their grasp and (2) opportunities extended to men must comport to some criterion that is relevant to the social welfare. The conservative complains that the social levelers, the popular democrats, are guilty of inducing bloated expectations that lead predictably to frustration, envy, and bitterness, and social Darwinists are to blame for recklessly disregarding social values and encouraging rapacious egocentrism.

5. Most conservatives attach more than a mere instructional value to social continuity or "tradition." The reason for this is their *teleological* view of the social experience. This viewpoint maintains that *purpose* underlies the historical narrative and ancient practice is authoritative in the sense that it embodies a purposive content. Burke called this phenomenon *prescription* and most twentieth century conservatives endorse one version of it or another. With some conservatives, this teleological motif is theocentric—as Burke once remarked that "history is the divine tactic." With others, the teleological factor has naturalistic origins. In either case, the conservative position stresses the integrity and even authority (if only heuristically) of each cultural or societal experience and warmly endorses cultural variety. At the same time, this cultural variation is not relativistic, since beyond the phenomena of each societal experience are the universals that undergird all human experience, be they transcendental or naturalistic. Thus, the mood of modern conservatism not only features a reverence for custom and tradition (as evidences of on-going purpose), but also an unmistakable cosmopolitanism, an absence of chauvinistic insularity.

There is in conservatism a revival of the pre-Christian conception of *piety*—a reverence for one's origins. Even such non-conservative writers as D. H. Lawrence, George Orwell, and Albert Camus have displayed this tendency. Religious orientations apart, conservatives argue for the need to have objects of reverence, even a sustaining social mystique, symbols endangered by the utilitarianism of the post-Industrial Revolution epoch. The principal source of these objects of reverence and myth is the social accumulation, the life-history of the race.

The teleological nature of tradition, its wisdom, is subrationally transmitted, in the opinion of many conservative theorists. The truths of the social experience are not discursive, they are not subject to direct rational penetration. They are conveyed in the realm of "feeling" or, perhaps, in psychic inheritance, an idea vaguely suggested by Burke, but given more substance by Nietzsche, Bergson, Freud, and Jung. The Romantic postulation of this notion, in Wordsworth, Coleridge, and

Goethe, for example, has taken on a far more explicit form in the twentieth century, relying on depth psychology and anthropology.

6. A primary jeopardy that was looming on the horizon of the twentieth century, in the opinion of Ortega y Gasset, was the "politicalization" of man. By that Ortega meant that man was increasingly construed to be a "political animal," but not in Aristotle's sense (which implied that the nature of man was inherently social or civil), but, rather, in terms of man's preoccupations being adequately subsumed within political ideology.

In various ways, twentieth century conservatives have sought to attack the idea of the primacy of politics. Quinton Hogg, in his *The Case for Conservatism,* indulged his British drollery by remarking that the conservative's first principle was "fun and foxhunting first." Others, less addicted, perhaps, to the sporting life of the English countryside, have suggested religion, art, and "high play" and even the more mundane joys of creaturehood as being activities of far vaster significance than politics. Michael Oakeshott has concluded that the fundamental role of government is "attending to the arrangements of society" and nothing more. This reduction of politics to a secondary, care-taking role in the affairs of men creates a certain tension in conservative thought regarding power, in general, and government, in particular. Unlike the nineteenth century liberals, twentieth century conservatives are not, in the main, proponents of weak government. But they are suspicious of concentrations of power; they are disquieted not only by government power, but also by economic and social power. Government (with its component of power) is, to conservatives, a necessary brake on potential social upheaval, the most formidable instrument of social control and, for the conservative, the maintenance of order is the first responsibility of government. Yet governments ought to be restricted in their applications of power, principally by ethical self-restraint and constitutional inhibitions. In essence, governments ought to be circumspect, they ought not to transgress the bounds of prudent discretion to tamper in areas inappropriate or unnecessary. But the only guarantee of this circumspection, the conservative maintains, is the quality of governmental leadership—not the right system, as Babbitt said, but the "right man." It is difficult, concludes the conservative, to generalize about power, to deal with it as an abstraction; power is dangerous in the wrong hands and useful and beneficial when exercised by the wise and self-disciplined.

Conservatives are more concerned about the qualitative dimensions of political leadership than are most popular democrats (due, likely, to their dismissal of the democrats' "tribunate" concept of leadership). Their attitudes toward leadership are markedly aristocratic: the ideal leader is motivated by a sense of public duty, is paternalistic in outlook, detached from social animosities, and the product of rigorous intellectual and ethical training. Most conservatives, again following Burke, suggest that, by and large, such leaders are apt to be recruited from a distinct social class that sponsors and inculcates these values. The ideal conservative leader is not, however, a "philosopher-king" or a professionalized governmental expert, as envisioned by Plato, Comte, or Herbert Simon. He preserves something of the aura of the amateur, since he, too, rejects the primacy of politics as a credo. The leader's function is, at once, both vital and modest, in the conservative view. His true strength lies in moral example.

7. Throughout the history of modern conservatism, including our century, there has been a noticeable penchant among conservatives for extolling the virtues of rural life, almost a sort of anti-urban orientation. The neo-Burkean defense of locality (the love for the "little platoon") seems invariably to imply, for contemporary conservatives, the locality as a rural hamlet, not a city neighborhood. For the most part, twentieth century conservatives have not endorsed an explicit agrarianism, but there seems a strong aesthetic preference for the beauty and tranquility of the countryside. It is probably true, historically speaking, that conservatives were the first "conservationists." Conservatism appears to be aware that the seat of aristocracy, at least in the Anglo-American tradition, has been the countryside. Closest examples to a bona fide American aristocracy have been based on landholding. Jefferson, certainly not a conservative, concluded that his "natural aristocracy" was best procured among the landed yeomanry. The European peasantry has been staunchly conservative—as Karl Marx well knew.

This preference for rural over urban values is indicative of conservatism's lack of anthropocentric hubris. Nature remains, for the conservative, the normative vision, perhaps inheriting this perspective from Aristotle and the Schoolmen. There is an affinity for natural forms that rebels against the deprivations perpetrated by the urban-technological epoch. The conservative preference for political flamboyance and even eccentricity (as in such figures as Burke, Randolph, Disraeli, and Churchill) is another facet of this romantic attachment to naturalistic sensualism. The chivalric *élan* of conservatism, still present in this century, bespeaks yet the attraction of the *beau sabreur,* the man acquainted with the verities of the natural drama.

From another direction, contemporary conservatism preserves a vivid tragic sense, eschatological and cultural. Its rhetoric, invariably powerful and replete with dark and awesome imagery, repeats the tragic theme, the motifs of birth, struggle, and death, so salient in nature. Its heroes are Oedipus, Lear, Faust, and Captain Ahab, juxtaposing tragedy and gallantry, a curious blend of hope and futility, of obedience, resignation, and perpetual aspiration.

THE ETHICAL ARGUMENT OF THE
CONSERVATISTS

The main impact of twentieth century conservatism has been its opposition to the growth of popular democracy. The primary attack mounted by traditionalist conservatives has been ethical in nature: the accusation that popular democracy is possible, but not desirable, because it debauches moral values. The cardinal faults of popular democracy are seen as moral relativism, licentiousness, mediocrity, and egocentricity.

But not all anti-democratic criticism has proceeded from these assumptions. Some critics have taken the position that democracy is not really a viable option, moral issues aside. These critics elect to argue that democracy, either substantively or procedurally defined, is illusory, impossible of attainment. The conjecture has been advanced that democracy is a premeditated hoax, a piece of political fraud. This viewpoint was vitriolically embroidered by H. L. Mencken, especially in his *Notes on Democracy*. Mencken, a self-proclaimed follower of Nietzsche, contended that the tenets of democracy were so contrary to nature as to be the products of fiction. He ridiculed the "common man" as "homo boobians" and "suckers" and declared them to be the victims of the cynical machinations of democratic politicians who were rogues and charlatans. Mencken's preference was for a leader more candidly a "strong man," the hero-leaders from the imaginations of Nietzsche and Carlyle: the Borgias, the Hohenstaufens, and the Percys. His final acerbic comment was that democracy is the "best" form of government because it is the most absurd and amusing.

The concept that democracy is an illusion, because political control inevitably is the province of the strong (those practitioners of the "will to power"), was related to the idea that social organization was inherently oligarchic. Much of this anti-democratic theory was predicated on the sociology of Pareto and Michels and upon the more aristocratically-oriented elitism of Mosca.

The conclusions of the European elitist sociologists influenced both fascist and non-fascist democratic critics in the United States. Among the former was Lawrence Dennis and among the latter,

James Burnham. As we have seen in chapter six, this elitist theory also influenced pro-democratic writers. To some degree, the difference between democratic and anti-democratic elitists was a matter of degree. The democratic elitists maintained that the social precepts of democracy required, for their survival, the existence of "democratic" elites (elites that accepted the procedural "rules" of democracy); the anti-democratic elitists replied that all elites responded to the imperatives of social organization and to consider a system constructed of elites irrevocably committed to democratic principles was an exercise in fantasy.

In large part, elitism, of both varieties, sprang up as a result of lowered evaluations of the political capabilities of the masses. Both the requisite native intelligence and the educability of men, en masse, was brought into serious question. The first instance of mass intelligence testing was undertaken by the U.S. Army in World War I and the results profoundly shocked many, even if the validity of these tests were ultimately successfully challenged. The American political scientist, E. M. Sait, was particularly discouraged regarding the feasibility of democracy as a result of the Alpha and Beta examinations.

Democrats and anti-democrats sharply divided on the potentialities of mass education. Democrats tended to be optimistic about the effects of education on political capacities, arising, largely, from their environmentalist convictions. Anti-democrats, on the other hand, were dubious about education as a means of increasing political judgment. Educational improvement could not alter, they contended, the natural dispersions of ability, and some libertarian-minded democratic critics were alarmed over the indoctrinational implications of mass education.

THE LIBERTARIANS

Not all those identified to the public at large as "conservatives" expressed these criticisms of democracy. Regardless of the niceties of nomenclature, those on the political Right who could be designated as "individualists" and "libertarians" were, in many respects, sympathetic to democracy. They were pluralists and advocates of an "open" society.

The origins of the individualists-libertarians were not conservative at all. They sponsored a revival of the spirit of nineteenth century liberalism; their intellectual forebears were J. S. Mill and, more particularly, Herbert Spencer and, in America, William Graham Sumner. Many were more or less orthodox social Darwinists. Their quarrel with twentieth century liberalism was that it had left the track; it had abandoned individualism for collectivism; it had ushered in the "welfare state," it had renounced the doctrine of laissez-faire.

These neo-liberal *libertarians* favored democracy, *if* by it was meant the maintenance of an open, mobile society constructed so as to insure individual prerogative. Popular democracy erred, in their view, when it reached the point of depriving individuals of their free-wheeling opportunities and their personally gained acquisitions. Some libertarians, like the American philosopher, John Hospers, blamed an aggrandizing government for this illegitimate encroachment on the freedom of the individual. This position, in turn, rejected the right of government to exercise authorities generally assumed to be a customary governmental preogative, such as conscripting citizens for the common defense, collecting taxes, and delivering the mail.

A defense of private property was a salient tenet of libertarianism. At heart, the advocates of this outlook were economic reductionists, the core of their position being free market economics. They argued that the principles of the free market were universally applicable to all aspects of society, not merely those explicitly economic in nature. Various forms of this viewpoint were expounded by "classical" economists like Ludwig von Mises and Frederic Hayek. The extreme extension of the libertarian position often merged into philosophical anarchy or took socially atavistic directions, as with the "objectivism" of the novelist, Ayn Rand.

The democracy envisioned by the libertarians was a bourgeois democracy, a social order predicated upon the supremacy of the entrepreneur. It was a democracy of opportunity and intellectual pluralism, but a democracy, also, that carefully avoided economic leveling and its social consequences. Such viewpoints bring contemporary libertarianism as a social theory, illustrated by the writings of Murray Rothbard, into sharp conflict with traditional conservatives and other democratic critics.

THE QUESTION OF "PERMANENT THINGS" IN THIS CENTURY

There is in contemporary conservatism an almost morose fear of a new Jacobin rising, an overt insurrection, perhaps a violent one, against the liberal, democratic hegemony. Conservatism, currently, views democratic liberalism as moribund and unable to sustain itself against the onslaught of new social radicalisms, which are even more objectionable to the conservatives than liberalism. This conservative, even "Tory," sense of alarm places its supporters in a difficult predicament: to go down with the "ship" of liberalism or to submit to the temptation of considering some counter-radicalism, in order to cope with the revolutionary ferment. In a sense, there has been a "radical" vein in the social thought of historical conservatism. Radical social reform is not unknown to the conservative persuasion, as can be evidenced in the social policies of Disraeli or Bismarck, but there is also an inclination to shore-up the defenses of the civilized order with an entente of more authoritarian shades of opinion. Moreover, conservatism in America does not know quite how to react to the mounting anger of the middle classes, the so-called "silent majority," with whom conservatives maintain only a remote attachment.

Contemporary critics have accused conservatism of Quixotism —a picturesque, if ineffectual, preference for the graces of the past. The conservative, evidently, is sensitive about "relevance" and what role he is to play in the drama of western politics. He feels his primary vocation is to recast what T. S. Eliot called the "permanent things" into the pertinent symbols of the century. But do these immutable truths exist and if they do has conservatism meaningfully recapitulated them? Is there a place for the noblesse oblige of the chivalric tradition in the age of nuclear power and the exploration of space?

FOR ADDITIONAL READING

BABBITT, IRVING, *Democracy and Leadership.* Boston: Houghton Mifflin, 1952 (orig. pub. 1924).

DE JOUVENEL, BERTRAND, *On Power: Its Nature and the History of Its Growth* (trans. by J. F. Huntington). Boston: Beacon Press, 1962 (orig. pub. 1945).

ELIOT, T. S., *Notes Toward a Definition of Culture.* New York: Harcourt, Brace, 1948.

KENDALL, WILLMORE, *The Conservative Affirmation.* Chicago: Henry Regnery, 1963.

KIRK, RUSSELL, *The Conservative Mind.* Chicago: Henry Regnery, 1953.

MORE, PAUL ELMER, *On Being Human.* Freeport, New York: Books for Libraries Press (Books for Libraries Communications), 1968 (orig. pub. 1936).

OAKESHOTT, MICHAEL, *Rationalism in Politics.* New York: Basic Books, 1952.

ORTEGA Y GASSET, JOSÉ, *The Revolt of the Masses* (trans. anonymous). New York: Mentor Books (New American Library), 1950 (orig. pub. 1930).

ROSSITER, CLINTON, *Conservatism in America.* New York: Knopf, 1956.

SANTAYANA, GEORGE, *Dominations and Powers.* New York: Scribner's, 1951.

VIERECK, PETER, *Conservatism Revisited.* New York: Collier Books (Macmillan), 1962 (orig. pub. 1949).

WEAVER, RICHARD, *Ideas Have Consequences.* Chicago: University of Chicago Press, 1948.

EIGHT

The Cry of Anguish

Existentialism

The term *existentialism* is more frequently heard in public conversation than in philosophical circles. It is a description more of a mood than a precise body of opinion. As a way of looking at the world, it appears to be distinctly apolitical, if not anti-social—it does not appear very interested in political and social questions, at least not on those terms usually applied to such issues. That is not surprising if one remembers that existentialism was a philosophical revolt and that the philosophical *Weltanschauung* it revolted against was inclined to give political and social questions high priority. Also, in its rejection of the prevailing philosophical orientations, existentialism wished to return to a consideration of individual human existence, to the problem of the *Existenz*, to devise philosophical means to gain an understanding of the intimate, personal Self.

However disdainful some existentialists were about conventional axiological philosophy, the effects of existentialism, as an intellectual mood, on ethical and social theory were considerable—

it declared, often in poignant and bitter terms, the sense of anguish and dread that crept into the culture late in the nineteenth century and reached its somber crescendo in the decades following the end of the Second World War. This anguish was sufficient, in some cases, to engender a feeling of futility, a cultural nihilism, profound enough to cause an overt rejection of social speculation and systematic political analysis.

At its beginnings, existentialism revolted against Hegelianism, especially Hegel's doctrine of "essences" or, more specifically, "essentialism." Beyond espousing the reality of essences, essentialism accorded to essences a far greater emphasis than it gave to the problem of existence. Existentialism sought to overturn this arrangement by announcing the primacy of existence. Such a broad attitude was also characteristic of the vitalists (see chapter two). Historically, however, the perspective of existentialism is identified with the Danish theologian, Søren Kierkegaard, whose life span roughly covered the first half of the nineteenth century. We need not be concerned with a detailed description of Kierkegaard's complex and elliptical thought, if only for the reason that it had a rather indirect impact on twentieth century existentialism. The Kierkegaardian legacy was in terms of his unusual blend of intense personalism, psychological commentary, poetic passion, religious mysticism, and an imminent sense of dread, anguish, and psychic terror. Frequently, the Kierkegaardian idiom would find a literary expression in the twentieth century, as with Jean Paul Sartre, Simone de Beauvoir, for example, or in the poetic theology of Martin Buber and Gabriel Marcel.

Existentialists are not at all sure about the nature of existence, probably because to frame an abstract concept of it would be to renounce its authenticity. Existence is "encountered," it is not conceptualized. This emphasis on personal encounter, the "existential crisis," results in widely differing tones of opinion regarding the significance of existence. At one end of the spectrum would stand Jean Paul Sartre whose views underscore a sense of futility, of hopeless anguish, of the final absurdity of the human predicament. "Phenomenological" existentialists, such as Martin Heidegger and Karl Jaspers, represent a more aloof approach in which the human situation is not irretrievable. Finally, there are the "Christian" existentialists, including Karl Barth and Nicholas Berdyaev, who, in differing ways, employ the perspectives of existentialism to re-examine the Christian position.

KARL JASPERS: A SEARCH FOR THE RE-ESTABLISHMENT OF ORDER

One of the earliest expressions of existentialism was the work of Karl Jaspers whose publication, in 1919, of *Psychology of World Views* is often cited as the beginning of twentieth century existentialism. Jaspers's roots are in Kierkegaard and Kant and, to some degree, he attempts a reconciliation between them. Initially, like Kierkegaard, Jaspers's thesis is the phenomenon of individual crisis, which he later extends to include cultural crisis. In Jaspers, the crisis is produced by intellectual limitations; man's comprehensions are inherently partial and ultimately unsatisfying, he seeks a complete explanation or truth (which Jaspers terms "encompassing"). While intellectually beyond his scope, this pursuit of truth is affected by a heightening of crisis, which produces a deeper intuitive feeling. This feeling is an awareness of the possibility of penetration into the Kantian *noumena*, the realm that was, for Kant, infinite and unknowable, the over-arching transcendental Being.

In terms of social philosophy, Jasper's conception of a multi-faceted freedom, of inevitable human social failure, and of a need for obedience prompts him not only to reject positivism and utopian social theory, but also to launch a counter-attack, principally directed against the rise of the mass-man, reflecting a Nietzschean influence, and technology. His views on these social matters are contained in his *Man in the Modern Age*, first published in 1931.

In a real sense, Jaspers's search is for the reestablishment of order, to find the roots of the "life-order." He finds the origins of human activity (although not explicitly of order) to be the state, mind, and humanity itself. The task, for him, is to relate these origins into a conscious and fundamental grasp of a satisfactory life-order. The predominant twentieth century configuration is a "technical life-order" that projects an attempt at mass rule. In *Man in the Modern Age*, Jaspers comments,

Even an articulated mass always tends to become unspiritual and unhuman. It is life without existence, superstition without faith. It may stamp all flat; it is disinclined to tolerate independence and greatness, but prone to constrain people to become as automatic as ants. (p. 40)

Such a life-order is incompatible with a "truly human life." "Truly human life," for Jaspers, is based upon the "claim to self-will and to existence (to self-expression)." Any life-order is limiting, but it is also one part of contact with or knowledge of reality, and it must be fused with the reality of human selfhood. The mass-ordered proclivities of advanced technology endanger this latter reality, merging the individual into the function. It also attempts, spuriously, to make this life-order absolute and static.

The reality of selfhood—the "authority of that being"—can only be actualized in the "real" world by the means of power. Writes Jaspers,

What man really becomes depends on the will of this power, which decides the historical concreteness of life in the whole. That power is at any time politically incorporated in the State and, as the tradition of historical human existence, it is education. (p. 89)

Jaspers speaks of a creation of a "state-will" which has two functions: (1) the direction of a life-order promoting the general welfare and (2) the creation of optimum or ideal conditions for creativity and the realization of possibilities. This concept of state function, argues Jaspers, constitutes no idolization of the state; the development of the ability to think politically entails a consciousness of the need for participation and the responsibilities of communal membership, but it also involves the preservation of independence from "surrender to a blind political will." Jaspers observes,

Selfhood begins with perplexity in the face of the real and the possible. The personal life vibrates in sympathy with the contemporaneous world processes, and increasingly clarifies its knowledge of the possible, until it becomes ripe to collaboration in the shaping of the situation. (p. 98)

Crucial to Jaspers's political outlook is leadership. The only alternative to the "struggle to secure a majority at the polls by means of propaganda, suggestion, humbug, and the advocacy of private interests" is the emergence of the "genuine leader," defined in terms of personal qualities of continuity and perspective. But such leaders are, contemporaneously, rare, leadership currently being comprised of "exponents of the transient will of the masses." Thus the essential idea of the state is negated and the sense of the state falls into decay. The emergence, on the other hand, of statist fanaticism and dictatorship also is a concept of leadership inharmonious with the expectations of humanity. The result is drift, indeed, a loss of faith in destiny.

The modern state, faced with the problem of education, has, asserts Jaspers, two alternative courses: (1) accept mass values as the basis of education or (2) attempt to counter these values of the massmen by an "aristocratic" educational program of its own. The first approach fails to meet the requirements of a culturally-unifying educational experience. The second is a threat to the freedom of the mind. The revival of genuine education, contends Jaspers, depends upon rejecting mass values by recognizing the difference between that which is "comprehensible to all" and that which can only be attained by an elite, who have disciplined and cultivated the Self.

How is modern man to preserve his vital selfhood in the contemporary predicament? Contemporary man, in Jaspers's view, is faced with a vast expansion of life possibilities. At the same time, however, he is affected by a sense of a drastic contraction of the breadth of his own intimate existential or self-expressive possibilities—"a sense of despair has affected human activity." There must be a new beginning, but it cannot rest upon a nihilistic retreat into subjective isolation, for it is only in community life that man attains self-knowledge, as Jaspers comments,

> Because selfhood exists only in unity with the being of the time, it is still resolutely determined to live only in this same time even though it should find itself in conflict therewith. Every act of its realization becomes the germ, however small, of the creation of a new world. (p. 217)

JEAN PAUL SARTRE: THE QUEST FOR
PERFECT FREEDOM

Jaspers's somewhat arisocratically-framed social outlook is not shared by all existentialists. Nor is his spiritualistic rejoinder to nihilism. A sharply different world-view is revealed by Jean Paul Sartre. Sartre served in the French Army from 1939 until his capture by the Germans in 1941. After his release he became a hero of the French resistance movement until 1944. Possessed with literary as well as philosophic talents, Sartre enjoyed wide success as a novelist and playwright. His major philosophical work, *L'Etre et le Néant (Being and Nothingness)* appeared in 1943.

The philosophy of Sartre is not easy for the layman to comprehend, at least not as it is presented in *Being and Nothingness*. Its subtitle, *Essay on Phenomenological Ontology*, gives some indication of the principle concerns of the work. In broad terms, Sartre's philosophy is a subjectivism in which the world is seen through the phenomenon of individual consciousness. This individual awareness or experience exhausts reality; Sartre reacts vigorously against the Kantian concept that something "real" exists behind, as it were, phenomena. In fact, Sartre's position is a solipsism. It denies, among other things, any substantial knowledge of another self. This failure of knowledge does not mean, however, that one individual is not struck by the realization of the existence of another. This other person, of whose existence one may be aware, represents another "world," another unique center of existence. As such, it constitutes a factor in the private grasp of existence and may even be a threat to it. Sartre supposes that the awareness of another in perception reduces that person to an "object," a conceptualization that the individual must overcome, as if it were an intrusion ultimately destructive, but at least productive of fear and shame. In this "conflict," the individual can, of course, reverse this subject-object relationship, insofar as cognition is concerned, or accept the "object" role. Sartre, in *Being and Nothingness*, is prone to cast these ideas of relationship in terms of a sexual explanation, the "sexual" as being the most obvious manifestation of the quest for existence. The struggle between individuals, the temporary survival of the freedom of one by the annihilation of the freedom of the other, sexually or otherwise, is eternally circular or endlessly irresolved, a condition that creates, in turn, a predicament of hopelessness, an inability to escape from the conflict or to find substantial satisfactions from human relationships.

In a way, Sartre's quest for existence is a quest for perfect freedom, but this freedom is apparently only realizable in total isolation from the invariably "inauthentic" human relationships, which, by definition, are threats to freedom. Choice, which is at the crux of freedom, must, for Sartre, be predicated upon the solipsistic view he takes of reality. "Hell," announces Sartre, "is other people."

It is not difficult to project a view of ethics and social thought from such a world-view. Freedom, in this sense, becomes virtually synonymous with ethical and social anarchy; it is a freedom without a shred of reciprocal restraint or commitment. The existentialism of Sartre, thus, cannot be said to explicitly imply an articulate political philosophy for the reason that the underlying assumptions are apolitical. And yet Sartre himself has, from time to time, taken an active interest in politics, espousing some esteem for Marxism. What Sartre endorses, however, is the revolutionary posture, per se. Such an outlook must arise, Sartre argues, because "man is unjustifiable." People are neither self- nor providentially-produced, all order can be transcended toward other orders, all prevailing values are reflections of the prevailing society, and society can be overturned in the interests of new, if barely perceived, societies.

Sartre's position finally is reducible to the proposition that the merit of revolution is that it is revolutionary. The chaos of revolution is to be preferred to order and stability, because it accords closer to the ideal of freedom. In more concrete terms, Sartre's enthusiasm for Marxism is not an endorsement of dialectical materialism (which Sartre rejects as an unsound philosophy). For Sartre, Marxism or communism is, momentarily, the most obvious and successful revolutionary vehicle. Such a viewpoint tends to deny the efficacy of social philosophy, save in the sense that social proposals are indications of inauthentic communications which, in Sartre's opinion, comprise virtually all human relationships.

ALBERT CAMUS: A SENSE OF THE ABSURD

Albert Camus was himself a tragic figure, prematurely dying in 1960, after having won the Nobel Prize in Literature in 1957. Born in Algiers in 1913, Camus lived to witness the unhappy events in his native country. He was by trade a litterateur, his fame resting upon belles lettres, but his novels and plays contain philosophical and political elements. As well, Camus was an essayist of merit. Particularly interesting are the essays in his collection, *The Myth of Sisyphus,* published in 1943.

A profound sense of the absurd pervades Camus' work, but this over-arching motif failed to produce in Camus the nihilistic reactions notable in some of his contemporaries. Indeed, Camus invariably displays a refreshing independence of attitude that culminates in a recognizable spirit of moderation, a refusal to be tempted by forms of philosophical and political extremism. Camus sought to discover the alternative to futile absurdity and he sought it not alone in the private confines of the individual psyche, but also in the patterns of social life. In short, Camus refused to jettison consideration of social and political responses to the existential predicament, nor did he choose to summarily discount the influences of historical experience. Camus was searching, probably in quite personal terms, for a sustaining rationale, some retort to the absurdity of existence other than abject resignation or bitter denunciation. This theme courses through all his novels, particularly *The Rebel.*

Camus was especially struck by the inhumanity man could inflict upon his fellows. He was witness to a time of horrors, not only World War II, but the cruelties of the Algerian conflict and other small but vicious struggles that took place in the world in the decades after Hiroshima. He clung to a belief in the importance and sanctity of individual human life and denounced the practice of cruelty. Yet the issues of life and death were but one aspect of the individual's effort to sustain himself. The value problem, admittedly, is stark when involved with those grim elementals, but to what standards do we repair in our daily lives in less imperative circumstances?

Camus represents a tension within the mood of French existentialism between philosophical anarchism and lingering regard for social order. Camus observes, in *The Myth of Sisyphus,* that "Sisyphus teaches a higher fidelity that negates the gods and raises rocks." But he goes on to add, "He too concludes that all is well, this universe henceforth without a master seems to him neither sterile nor futile." A "higher fidelity" to what? Camus sees the universe "without a master." His rejection of the idea of a "master" is not a mere statement of atheistic preference, but an announcement that no objective order exists to which allegiance is due. The "higher fidelity" is wholly personalistic and involves the "absurd victory," the recognition of one's ultimately hopeless predicament, the purport of the retelling of the ancient myth of Sisyphus' punishment by the gods.

Camus' affirmation is the "yes" that is said by the absurd man who knows and accepts his personal fate. Not much is left, consequently, of the social fabric other than its being the arena of the discovery of the absurdity of life. Camus' denunciation of the forces oppressing men, the crushing weight of inhumanity, finally summons forth an anarchistic quietism in which individual men can only survive by recognition of their fate, by resignation and non-participation in the motivations and devices of oppression.

EXISTENTIALISM: NEW PERSPECTIVES

The principal effect of existentialism on contemporary social thought is anthropological, providing new angles of perspective from which to deal with the problem of man. The very elemental nature of the existentialist posture, its subjectivism, lends itself to this orientation. Indeed, existentialism has made an imprint on contemporary psychology, a movement called *existential psychotherapy.* A chapter in Sartre's *Being and Nothingness* is entitled "Existential Psychoanalysis." Prominent in applying the orientations of existentialism to psychotherapy is Rollo May, author of *Existential Psychology,* published in 1961. May reasserts the Sartrian viewpoint when he states that the therapy situation begins with the assumption that the patient "is centered in himself and an attack on this centeredness is an attack on his existence." He goes on to define "neurosis" as a "distortion of this need for centeredness." Other sources of existentialist psychology are found in the works of Merleau-Ponty, Joseph Lyons, and Medard Boss. In wider-based anthropological terms, the work of Paul Ricoeur is central. Ricoeur's basic thesis (to be found in his article, "The Antinomy of Human Reality"*) begins with the statement of a problem, the problem of understanding man as "fallible," being "suspended between a pole of infinitude and a pole of finitude"; man, as Descartes put it, "is like a mean between being and nothingness"—hence, the title of Sartre's major opus. For Ricoeur, man is seen as being highly "fragile."

Looking at man in this way, it is possible to understand his prephilosophical comprehension, the origin of his myths which are in reality statements derived from pathos or what Ricoeur calls the "pathos of misery" arising from his primordial fragility and incompleteness. This prephilosophical, prerational comprehension was not only the genesis of philosophy, but was also a knowledge of unusual completeness, a knowledge that philosophy can state in rational terms, but cannot transcend. Such a thesis links Ricoeur to a large-based anthropological concern for the nature and function of myth, as is found, in varying versions, in the speculations of Erich Neumann and Joseph Campbell and the religious historian, Mircea Eliade.

Ricoeur is primarily concerned with the passage from the mythic to the philosophical understanding—from *mythos* to *logos*. He conceives this metamorphosis in stages, the first of which he contends develops from the "transcendental imagination," the ability to objectify the world and to reflect. Thus man does not merely "receive" the external world, but seeks to penetrate it and understand it. This affects man's internalized dichotomy, for reflection presumes an "intentionality." This "intentionality" is vital to man's ability to relate the external world in such a way as to produce order and synthesis, and it develops a new unity. Never lost, how-

* Paul Ricoeur, "The Antinomy of Human Reality and the Problem of Philosophical Anthropology," in *Readings in Existential Phenomenology*, eds. N. Laurence and D. O'Connor (Englewood Cliffs, N.J.: Prentice-Hall, Inc., 1967), pp. 390–402.

ever, is the enduring theme of primordial pathos. A proper philosophical anthropology is conceived by Ricoeur to be a combination of the "precomprehension of pathos" and the "rigor of the transcendental method."

In pursuing this objective, Ricoeur invokes a doctrine of "feeling." Feeling, for Ricoeur, is the most general function in the constitution of the person, the most intense focus of human fallibility. It is also the reverse of the "objectification" of the transcendental imagination. Comments Ricoeur, "The function of feeling is to 'reincorporate' into the vital depths what has been thus 'removed' from the depths of life." This does not imply the hostility of feeling and knowledge or internalization and objectification. Ricoeur considers them as contemporary: "They are born together and grow together," he concludes. Feeling is mediation if it represents a close connection with the counterpart of knowledge; it is, in Ricoeur's words, "the zone of transition from simple vitality to pure spirituality." Feelings, actualized as passions, are a guide, then, to the primordial demands of human nature, even if they are objectified by the transcendental imagination. But to understand these passions as they are regulated by "intentional objects," one must conceive of them in terms of a transcendental a priori structure.

The passions form a mediation between corporeal and spiritual life. They constitute the ground for the self-conscious Self, separate from other objects. The essential "fragility" of man arises from the means by which the demands of the passions are satisfied. Ricoeur, viewing the passions as the synthesis of the vital and the spiritual, suggests that the termination of the vital demands is *pleasure* and of the spiritual demands, *happiness*. These demands may be inexhaustible; even happiness is not fully enduring. Mankind features, then, a perpetual restlessness, a disharmony, perhaps provoked by an inability to know what is enough, an inability to conceptualize a complete satisfaction of the demands of the passions.

The processes of need, development, and completion are invariably open-ended and on-going. Conceptions of this cycle of desire are never complete or fixed. No problematic orientation will suffice; utilitarianism is sterile. Ricoeur comments, in "The Antinomy of Human Reality,"

The reducing of actions to techniques and the postponements of the self's goal contribute to the feeling of insecurity and emptiness, which often pervades human action.

The passions, rather, serve as the means of relationship between the vital and the spiritual, but this realm of feeling is also the scene of conflict. Ricoeur summarizes,

> The initial pathos, reduced by transcendental reflection, is recovered in a theory of praxis and feeling. But the preunderstanding of pathos is inexhaustible. That is why philosophical anthropology is never completed. Above all it is never done with its task of recovering the irrationality of its nonphilosophical source in the rigor of reflection. Its misfortune is not to be able to save both the depth of pathos and the coherence of logos.

EXISTENTIALIST ANTHROPOLOGY

The existentialist literature pertaining to philosophical anthropology, while it preserves the motif of dread or pathos and the invocation of the subjective predicament, discloses marked cleavages in existentialist thought. Deep differences of view regarding the presence and nature of a spiritual dimension and the potentialities of man and society are evident. In a somewhat more restricted sense, existentialist anthropology reveals certain important general tenets regarding: (1) the nature of human action; (2) the nature of the Self; and (3) the historical situation of man.

1. Ricoeur's theory of "feeling" is similar to other writers' concern for emotion, and their assumption that the emotional life of man is purposive and not merely coincidental in the human psyche. Human preoccupations—such as happiness, hope, and even death —take on new and amplified significance in existentialist thought.

2. The picture of the Self, in existentialist literature, becomes increasingly relational rather than static. This relational concept of the Self is multi-faceted, involving perceptual, ontological, and interpersonal relationships. What constitutes the inner core of the person must be considered in relation to the intricate fabric of phenomena in which the Self drifts.

3. By rejecting a concept of history as a mere sequence of events, existentialist anthropology sees the human situation *in* history as one of a consciousness of a past linked to a consciousness of the indeterminancy of a future. Such a view underscores the almost terrifying burden of choice in regard to the dispositions of future action.

All these considerations combine into an over-riding anxiety for human survival, a survival that is not evaluated solely in terms of physical catastrophe. The social and political focus of existentialism has been to frame responses to the question of what is "humanness" and how is it best preserved. Reactions to this question provoke attitudes both radical and conservative in outlook, witness the contrast between Sartre and Jaspers. Existentialism's difficulty, ultimately, in positing more or less explicit types of political and social philosophy, arises from its conviction that the root crisis of the twentieth century human is spiritual. In which case, how does one transliterate the crisis and torment of the spirit into the vocabulary of political and social alternatives?

CHRISTIAN EXISTENTIALISM

An aspect of existentialism that attempts to resolve the spiritual problem is so-called *Christian existentialism*. This movement is a resurfacing of the Augustinian tradition in religious thought. It places primary emphasis upon the existential relationship of man and God—the "I–Thou" relationship, in the terminology of Marcel and Buber. It is not surprising, then, that existentialism was allied with the neo-orthodox movement in Protestant theology, e.g., Barth, Tillich, and Niebuhr, and with the distinctly modified neo-Thomist orientations of Etienne Gilson and Jacques Maritain, among Catholics. Christian existentialism certainly encouraged a movement away from natural theology, but it also ranged against historicism and social gospelism. It sought to view religion in terms of ways in which the human–God relationship was perceived and related.

The Christian existentialist movement is pertinent to social philosophy in two ways: (1) it shares the existentialist concern with personal crisis, dread, and the need for concern with the immediate spiritual predicament; and (2) it rejects nihilistic and atheistic responses to this predicament by repostulating religion as the only viable means of escape from the absurdities of existence.

The writings of many theologians and religiously-grounded philosophers, under existentialist influence, contain a theme of pessimism and reproach regarding contemporary social life, as in Marcel and Niebuhr. Also, however, they contain a reaffirmation of spiritual hope based upon the general desecularization of society. Of the Christian existentialists directly interested in social philosophy, this viewpoint is succinctly expressed by Nicholas Berdyaev, who emerges from the tradition of Eastern Orthodoxy, the intellectual tradition of the Russian church. Berdyaev was appalled by both the carnage of World War I and the sterility and instability of the philosophical climate that followed it. He was a dedicated historian (as is testified to by such works as *The Meaning of History* and *The Russian Revolution*), as well as a theologian whose work, *Christian Existentialism,* is an illuminating discussion. Berdyaev's excursion into social thought was his *The Fate of Man in the Modern World,* published in English in 1935. In it, he offers a comprehensive analysis of what he called "new forces in the world," including fascism and communism. He also extends a critique of liberal democracy and what he believes is its destructive effect on humanism:

> This democratized and generalized humanism has ceased to be attentive to man: it is interested in the structure of society, but not in man's inner life. This is a fatal and inevitable process. (p. 26)

Man is dehumanized, he asserts, to the extent of being reduced to the bestial, either by the rapacious forces of totalitarianism or by the spiritually barren, but fashionable philosophies of the era. In part, this is because, concludes Berdyaev, "we live in an epoch of plebeian revolt against every aristocratic element in culture." The rise of mass culture means the shift of emphasis from the spiritual, to the material and the vulgar. The restoration of a "humanistic culture" based upon aristocratic values is no longer practicable, he argues, and, instead, our hope must lie in what he terms a "religious renaissance." "This alone," he contends, "is capable of solving the problem of the right relationships between the aristocratic and the democratic, the personal and the social elements in culture."

This history of Christianity, Berdyaev observes, is a history of successes and failures, temptations, and erroneous judgments, and it has often obfuscated the direct confrontation of man with God. Harsh indictments are now being made against historical Christianity. Whether or not such condemnations are deserved, for Berdyaev, the sum result is grim:

> The world is again in the grip of the polydemonism from which Christianity once rescued it. DeChristianization led to dehumanization, and this to insanity, since the very image of man is darkened. (p. 126)

Berdyaev calls for a new "piety," a "mobilization of the spirit," in contrast to a preoccupation with social systems and reforms. This piety is not wholly concerned with an upward-moving love of God, but also with a revived reverence for man and the natural order. There is an emphasis not on salvation alone, but with worldly creativity. Berdyaev asserts,

> This problem of man takes precedence over that of society or of culture, and here man is to be considered, not in his inner spiritual life, not as an abstract spiritual being, but as an integral being, as a being social and cosmic as well. (p. 130)

PHILOSOPHICAL VALUES OF EXISTENTIALISM

In the last analysis, the philosophical value of existentialism has been two-fold: (1) to reintroduce, particularly in social thought, a much-needed emphasis upon the tragic, if not the absurd, motif in human existence, heretofore unresolved by the rationalistic or scientific method; (2) it has served a critical function by liberating philosophical reflection from the confines of intellectual convention. This latter situation is nicely summed up by the American philosopher, John Wild, in his *The Challenge of Existentialism*:

The world as it is concretely and immediately given to us, as presented with constraining evidence, is neglected. It is no wonder that the resulting world perspectives are partial, one-sided, and out of touch with common experience. Modern philosophy has paid too much attention to the tools of logic and analysis and the building of vast constructive systems, and far too little to the wide ranges of immediate data that lie beyond the province of the restricted sciences. This is a primary reason for the breakdown of philosophy. (pp. 15–16)

Existentialism and, collaterally, phenomenology have sought to remedy the condition described by Wild, and in doing so, have injected a sense of urgency and a humanistic sensitivity into the corpus of twentieth-century political life.

FOR ADDITIONAL READING

BLACKHAM, H. J., *Six Existentialist Thinkers.* New York: Harper, 1959.

BERDYAEV, NICHOLAS, *Christian Existentialism* (trans. by D. A. Lowrie). New York: Harper, 1965.

BUBER, MARTIN, *The Eclipse of God: Studies in the Relation Between Religion and Philosophy.* New York: Harper, 1952.

CAMUS, ALBERT, *The Rebel.* New York: Vintage Books (Random House), 1956.

GRENE, MARJORIE, *Introduction to Existentialism.* Chicago: University of Chicago Press, 1948.

HEINEMAN, F. H., *Existentialism and the Modern Predicament.* Bloomington: Indiana University Press, 1955.

JASPERS, KARL, *Man in the Modern Age* (trans. by E. and C. Paul). New York: Anchor Books (Doubleday), 1957 (orig. pub. 1931).

LAUER, QUENTIN, *Phenomenology: Its Genesis and Prospect.* New York: Harper, 1965 (orig. pub. 1958).

MERLEAU-PONTY, MAURICE, *The Primacy of Perception and other Essays.* Evanston: Northwestern University Press, 1964.

RICOEUR, PAUL, *Fallible Man.* Chicago: Henry Regnery, 1965.

SARTRE, JEAN PAUL, *Being and Nothingness* (trans. by Hazel Barnes). New York: Washington Square Press (Simon & Schuster), 1966 (orig. pub. 1953).

WILD, JOHN, *The Challenge of Existentialism.* Bloomington: Indiana University Press, 1955.

NINE

The Revolutionary
Enthusiasm

The New Radicalism

The twentieth century has seen many radical ideologies. Communism and fascism, certainly radicalisms, were mass movements of enormous scope. Each age has had its quota of social theories that demand the virtual abolition of present practices in favor of the institution of alternative ones. Some of these movements were, frankly, picturesque, some deadly serious, and a few committed to the attainment of their objectives by almost any means, to include violence and terror.

The radicalisms that followed World War II had some unusual characteristics. In the first place, only a small portion of them were direct outgrowths of earlier mass radical movements, such as Marxist communism. Many of them represented the agitation of ethnic and national groups arising from either actual or imagined states of repression. Increasingly, the radical mood permeated classes of people who formerly were not disposed to advocate a drastic alteration of the status quo—radicalism was no longer the cast of mind of intellectuals and proletarians only. Finally, the wave of radical sentiment that marked the 1950s and '60s featured a noticeable moralism, a reappearance of argument regarding rudimentary human values.

The main cockpit of this radical agitation was the United States. This was not surprising in view of the fact that the Cold War had juxtaposed an institutionalized radicalism, communism, against the "Free World," dominated economically and militarily by the United States. This international state of affairs served as the backdrop for the social and political issues that rent the American status quo in the period since 1950, and the surrogates of those issues have reverberated throughout the non-communist world, especially Western Europe. Indeed, the confrontation of the super powers, the USA and the USSR, heightened the proclivity of this new radicalism to find social inspiration in other places, in the thought of Mao, for example, or the revolutionary romanticisms suggested by the emerging "Third World" of non-aligned and "under-developed" states.

There was one feature of the new radicalism that was particularly singular: it proceeded more from a sort of adumbrated feeling than it did from either intellectual leadership or, more or less, systematic social philosophy. It produced slogans and heroes that were amalgams of the past, eclectic borrowings. The heroes of the new radicalism revealed no particular skein of philosophical consistency; they included Marx, Trotsky, Mao, Che Guevara, Gandhi, Martin Luther King, Jean Paul Sartre and, on occasion, St. Francis and Jesus Christ. Radicalism had few philosophically articulate spokesman, save, perhaps, Herbert Marcuse and Merleau-Ponty. Its literature was primarily to be found in manifestoes, placards, "underground" publications, predominantly polemical, and "transcriptions" of mass rallies.

A THROWBACK TO ROUSSEAU

The very confusing nature of what constituted the philosophical base of the new radicalism provides an initial clue to its underlying *Geist*. It was a new manifestation of irrationalism, the triumph of the emotion over reason, a resurgence of the spirit of

Rousseau. The revolutionary thrust of the new radicalism—intellectually or politically—may be best understood against the background of Rousseau's ideas. Reacting to the excesses of the social system produced by the Industrial Revolution, the demolition of sustaining social institutions and mystiques, and the physical insecurities of the post-nuclear international order, the genesis of the new radicalism was, in fact, a quest for simplicity, a revival of the pastoral virtues, a reaffirmation of earthy sensuality, an angry rejection of the complexities and sophistications of the twentieth-century world.

It thus took the image of a youth movement. The model society was the bucolic "commune." In fact, some observers, like Theodore Roszak, referred to this social agitation as the creation of a "counter-culture." Whether or not this designation is an accurate invocation of the term "culture," the opposition to the prevailing cultural patterns were extremely diversified—from the quasi-existentialism of the "Beats" to the active social revolutionaries of a more doctrinaire sort. In fact, a primary division in this new radicalism could be made between those who were essentially apolitical to those highly motivated by express political considerations. Considerable bitterness was evidenced between those who adopted a "drop out" point of view toward the culture, and those deeply committed to revolutionary action proceeding from well-delineated ideological convictions, such as those who proposed to march under the ideological banner of the late Leon Trotsky. By the late 1960s, even Herbert Marcuse, the supposed intellectual progenitor of political radicalism in America, was considered, in some quarters, to be too aloof, uncommitted and negativistic in attitude.

In the 1960s, it became common to refer to this new radicalism in more or less conventional political terminology; it was designated as the *New Left*. But the implicit category is confusing, since the New Left embraces a complex assortment of social forces. In a manner of speaking, the New Left emerged as a coalition of four major currents: (1) radicalized elements of the Old Left; (2) ideological revolutionaries, such as Maoists and Trotskyites; (3) minorities concerned with various specific objectives, e.g., black power, women's liberation; (4) special interest groups, largely counter-cultural and concerned with the cultivation of alternative life-styles, e.g. advocates of drugs, sexual liberation, and extreme forms of ecological preservation.

These groups would, on occasion, conjoin on specific issues, such as the Indo-China War, conscriptions, or civil rights. But on a philosophical level, tensions were apparent, ranging from a preference for various forms of social anarchism to highly systematized social theories. Again, to some, a counter-culture implied a free, hedonistic mode of life. To others, it meant puritanical dedication and group discipline. But to all, it meant the overthrow, by neglect or revolution, of the existing social order.

ROOTS OF MILITANCY

In large measure, this new social radicalism, particularly among the young, dates from the confrontations regarding race that took place in the United States in the 1950s. The post-World War I period had seen youthful enthusiasms for pacifism and social nihilism, but the conflict over racial equality, the civil rights movement, brought radical momentum to the fore, served as a catalyst, and such energies were transmitted to Europe, as well.

Black anger became a rallying point for social dissatisfaction more widely based. It provided an almost romantic, evangelistic sense of identification for non-black elements of the New Left, as well. The voices of this black protest were admired in direct proportion to their degree of militancy and recherché images: Malcom X, Stokely Carmichael, and Eldridge Cleaver. A unique literature was produced by these black militants, such as Malcom X's autobiography and Cleaver's *Soul on Ice*. This racial preoccupation was quickly seen as a global inequity in which the peoples of the "Third World," although possibly superior in virtue, were distinctly inferior in terms of their share of the world's goods. Frantz Fanon's *The Wretched of the Earth* became a popular text. The revolutions of the world's down-trodden became models for the emancipation of the oppressed or allegedly oppressed minorities in the industrialized societies. The social programs of Mao and Castro were held up as guides to the revolutionary aspirations of

Americans and Europeans. American racial inequalities were linked to the world-wide phenomenon of "imperialism."

Two somewhat singular features were characteristic of this militancy:

1. Although it was prone to employ the vocabulary of Marxism (and to pay a rather remote homage to Marx himself), it was not merely an extension of the Marxist-Leninist philosophy. Some committed Marxists, even active workers in the communist cause, were among the new radicals, such as Herbert Aptheker, the American communist, but their numbers were small and their motives occasionally suspected. A more sizeable segment of the movement, under the standard of the Young Socialists Alliance, were inspired by the somewhat neglected ideas of Leon Trotsky, who had been an assassination victim of Stalin's secret police.

   But while the new radicals approved of some of the ideas of Marx, especially those condemning capitalism, their philosophical base was hardly dialectical materialism. Most of the new radicals disowned it to the extent that they knew about it. The new radicalism was not a form of economic reductionism.

2. The new radicalism was not a proletarian movement. Indeed, most of the conventionally-defined "working classes" were in opposition to it, especially in the United States. Trade unionism, devoted to a social democratic viewpoint and intimately associated with the old, gradualistic, socialistic Left, reacted in a bluntly hostile manner. The new radicals—young militants and New Left theorists—were largely recruited from either self-conscious ethnic minorities or, even to a larger extent, from the middle classes where they represented a disaffected element. Even the overt battlegrounds of revolutionary confrontation were not factories and street barricades, but universities and political conventions, appendages of the bourgeois society.

There were still other characteristics of the new radicalism that underscored its uniqueness. One was an uneasiness about engaging in conventional philosophical discourse, attempts to persuade by evidence or rational demonstration. Many of the New Left argued that to do so was to play into the hands of their erstwhile adversaries by acknowledging the primacy of reason. In any case, many radicals thought such forms of argument to be sterile and inauthentic; they ranged too far from the imperative of feeling. This supremacy of the emotion was highly characteristic of forms of radicalism that espoused an ethnic mystique or reiterated some concept of the "general will" in neo-Rousseauistic terms. To be "relevant" was to abandon the abstractions of esoteric philosophical discussion and to address directly matters political and social. The irrationalist vein in the new radicalism, strangely like fascism, was thought to unite action and thought, with a categorical priority given to the former.

An illustration of this orientation is Tom Hayden's *Port Huron Statement,* 1962, an interesting articulation of the new radicalism and one connected with the younger militants, especially the Students for a Democratic Society that, during the late 1960s, waged a program of agitation on university campuses. Yet, more or less formal theoreticians did have a significant impact on contemporary radical thought and two of these major writers may serve as useful illustrations of this outlook: Frantz Fanon and Herbert Marcuse.

FRANTZ FANON

Growing directly out of the consciousness of race and the restlessness created by nineteenth century colonialism was the Algerian psychiatrist, Frantz Fanon. Born in the French Antilles in 1925, Fanon was educated in France and became a resident of Algeria. He supported the FLN rebels in that country and eventually left his practice of psychiatry to devote his full energies to the pan-African independence movement and the revolutionary cause of those peoples he considered to be oppressed. He died of leukemia in 1961, the same year that saw the publication of his most influential work, *Les damnés de la terre*—published in English under the title *The Wretched of the Earth,* in 1965.

The most prominent theme in Fanon's writings is racial consciousness, particularly "negritude." His awareness of the significance of racial origins, the social gulfs it creates, the political subjugations and confrontations it provokes merges in his later writings with a more cosmopolitan endorsement of revolutionary socialism. There is an evident metamorphosis in Fanon's thought from the predominantly intellectual preoccupations with the phenomenon of racial consciousness (which exhibit his psychiatric background) and his interests in French philosophy, particularly Sartre's existentialism, to the militancy, the harshly adversarial tone he finally adopts in his last work.

The Wretched of the Earth is ostensibly a revolutionary tract, written against the background of the Algerian conflict, to which the book makes numerous references. It is a work that sought to provide a revolutionary rationale, not for the European proletariat, but for the masses of the other continents, particularly Africa. This preoccupation causes Fanon to depart almost totally from traditional Marxist thought; his conceptions of socialism are broad and eclectic, constructed upon the singular cultural configurations of the "under-developed" regions. The revolution is against colonialism, actual or submerged.

Departing from his earlier more intellectual predilections, *The Wretched of the Earth* comes close to being a paean in praise of the revolution of social primitives, the most "wretched" of the culture—Marx's *Lumpenproletariat* becomes, for Fanon, the important revolutionary element. Three principal motifs emerge: (1) the rural base of the revolution; (2) the nationalistic character of the revolution; (3) the indispensability of violence.

There is, for Fanon, no need for a revolutionary vanguard of ex-bourgeois intellectuals. There is, indeed, little sympathy for the nominally constituted proletariat. The remaking of the world must fall to the simple workers of the rural areas and, equally, to the social outcasts who will in the cataclysm of violent revolution both discover their latent psyches, enhance their statures as persons, and provide the insights required to bring the revolution to fruition. The struggle, Fanon's conception of class warfare, is not economic, but involves the clash and triumph of ethnic identity and liberation from the constraints of psychological subjugation.

The world revolution, as envisioned by Fanon, becomes highly nationalistic. Indeed, the concept of nationhood is seen as a vital check against the eruption of tribalism. The nation is the key factor in the emergence of "identity," which is the primary aim and result of the revolutionary enterprise.

This emphasis on the appearance of a new "soul," a new awareness of the significance of existence needed by subservient peoples, is apparent in Fanon's vigorous endorsement of violence. Revolutionary violence is not for him simply a means to an end; it is not an operational concept. Violence is an irreplacable catalytic experience, necessary to the discovery of the individual and national psyche. No liberation is therefore possible without the almost ritualistic phenomenon of massive violence.

Out of this violent ordeal was to spring, in Fanon's vision, not only a new consciousness, but also a new political entity that would not crystallize into party control or personal dictatorship. Instead it would preserve, as an on-going characteristic, the *élan* of the revolutionary crucible. Finally, therefore, Fanon depicts a social order based upon the concept of the infinite revolution, the never-ceasing convolutions of revolutionary energies.

HERBERT MARCUSE

Considered by many as the leading theoretician of the New Left is Herbert Marcuse. Born in Berlin in 1898, Marcuse repaired to the United States in 1934, where he has remained. Marcuse's early interests were in the philosophy of Hegel. He early displayed a lively dislike for positivism. His enthusiasm for Hegelian philosophical detachment did not, however, extend to an admiration of post-Hegelian phenomenology, and Marcuse turned to Marx, especially his philosophy of history, as a possible alternative to both positivism and phenomenology. Also apparent in Marcuse's early work was a hedonistic predilection that eventually manifested itself in Marcuse's attention to Freud and his effort to reconcile Marxist and Freudian precepts, especially in his *Eros and Civilization*, published in 1955.

What had Marcuse seen in Marx? Certainly, Marcuse's philosophic position was never an explicit espousal of dialectical materialism. Marx, from Marcuse's point of view, had observed the two-layered nature of culture in which the paradigms of the future were manifest beneath the ostensible configurations of existent cultural life. Marx not only presented a new glimpse of reality for Marcuse, but also introduced a novel explanation of historical determinism.

Marcuse's fascination with Freud seems more difficult to explain, although it has been suggested that Marcuse saw in Freud a systematic social psychology, which classical Marxism lacked. The explanation probably lies in the fact that Marcuse conceived that at least some aspects of Freud's theory could be employed, properly re-interpreted, as a part of Marcuse's critique and denunciation of existing culture. In *Eros and Civilization,* the point of attack was the bourgeois "work ethic" and the Freudian-*cum*-Marcusean counter-hypothesis was the "pleasure principle."

Although Freud's "pleasure principle" invokes a psychological hedonism, it was but one element in his basic assumption of a vital balance between sexual demands and civilized restraints. Marcuse, on the other hand, elected to advocate libidinal liberation, the employment of erotic or "pleasure" forces as a means of radical social reformulation. Put another way, repression for Freud was an indispensable factor in the maintenance of society. Marcuse, alternatively, argues that repression is only the result of specific historical circumstances and that the economic and material advancement now renders repression superfluous. Yet it is paradoxical in the closing portions of *Eros and Civilization* that Marcuse, having put the "work ethic" to rest and the "pleasure principle" in its stead, feels the need to enforce sexual liberation by similar means of coercion, which he evidently dislikes, when used to support the "work ethic."

Marcuse's most widely-read works came considerably after *Eros and Civilization. One-Dimensional Man* appeared in 1964, *Negations* in 1968 and *An Essay on Liberation* a year later. Certain stylistic difficulties (in the view of some critics) notable in Marcuse's earlier works become more apparent in the later works which are candidly polemical. *One-Dimensional Man* is uneven and lacks a certain unity; the other volumes that follow it are brief and somewhat erratic. These faults notwithstanding, Marcuse's work forms a significant part of the literature of the new social radicalism.

One-Dimensional Man is an ambitious work designed to level a bill of indictment against contemporary society. Marcuse fills the volume with condemnations of cultural life, largely American culture. The main thesis of the book is that all progressive change, dissent, and even meaningful thought is now impossible within society. This condition is seen as a result of a conspiratorial merger of social forces, made possible by technological advancement. Economic accomplishment, affluence, has only produced the satisfaction of "false" needs, but has neglected and often repressed real needs. Consumption, at the levels produced in American society, have simply "bought off" the protest that should and would follow from a deeper sense of need. The potentially revolutionary proletariat is lulled into compliance with the purposes of entrenched exploiter classes by the technique of stimulating "false" needs and satisfying them. All aspects of life, sexuality and art, for example, contends Marcuse, lose their deeper significances and become facets of an over-riding social control that creates, in its turn, a "one-dimensional" culture.

Marcuse does not limit his attack to social patterns; he also condemns contemporary thought, the alleged sterility of conventional rationality. He espouses, instead, a variety of primitive irrationalism, a recrudescence of the domination of the instincts over disciplined reflective thought, an argument he continues to pursue in his other works, especially *An Essay on Liberation*. There is, however, a somewhat curious twist to Marcusean irrationalism: the final pages of *One-Dimensional Man* disclose a preference for a vague sort of ethical absolutism, the obliquely suggested existence of some objective realm of values, presumably to be known not only through the unleashing of the instincts, but also discoverable through the experience of cultural insurgency.

The response to the ultimately intolerable conditions of contemporary life, in Marcuse's view, is revolution, the violent demolition of the culture, instigated, at least initially, by the most deracinated and rejected elements of that culture. The potentialities of this societal insurrection are disclosed in such works as *Negations, An Essay on Liberation,* and Marcuse's contribution to *A Critique of Pure Tolerance,* with Barrington Moore, Jr. and Robert Paul Wolff. In fact, the tone of pessimism—or at least dubious progress —in *One-Dimensional Man* is replaced by a free-wheeling, almost futuristic enthusiasm. The revolutionary thrust is distinctly psychologistic; human nature can be remade (and, hence, society reconstituted) by the destruction of existing social limitations and by a new recognition of human needs. Marcuse redefines these human needs in essentially biological terms. This biologism, in Marcuse, follows from a highly speculative view of the natural order itself, largely unaffected by current empirical investigations of nature. There is, in fact, an obvious tension between an outlook that stresses the malleability of man, his susceptibility to premeditated conditioning, and some view of a "natural" configuration of the human psyche. In short, Marcuse's view of nature and of the natural factors in human nature are at once both primitivistic and aloof from the broad naturalistic conceptions of contemporary cultural anthropology. He presumes a sort of rudimentary harmony and egalitarianism that has now been corrupted by post-industrial societies. Only the dispossessed, so to speak, retain any contact with these past simplicities, such as Chinese peasants or American slum-dwellers. Hence, these social elements not only possess the true social insights, but must also be the revolutionary advanced guard of the new culture.

Marcusean biologism reveals a preference for a social order resting upon absolute values in contrast to nominal definitions of freedom. In his much-discussed essay, "Repressive Toleration," Marcuse seeks to demonstrate that the pluralistic and relativistic orientations of democracy amount to a false-front masking a latent repression. A reprehensible majority, he argues, uses the devices of democratic practice, such as freedom of speech, to enforce its will and to suppress protest and the wisdom of alienated minorities. Marcuse is willing, therefore, to engage in repression himself, so long as it is in the service of a subjectively-delineated truth. Conventional conceptions of freedom of expression and choice are intolerable, since they are too readily exploitable by ideologically-tainted majorities who have not been exposed to the liberating influences inherent in atavistic sensitivity.

Sensitivity, to the underlying instinctual summons, quite arbitrarily designated by Marcuse, is, at once, the key to both the new society Marcuse seeks to create and to the revolutionary phalanx he conceives to be the means of its attainment. Marcuse's description of this revolutionary coalition is somewhat perplexing. Its composition appears not to rest upon the common characteristics ordinarily used by social theorists. Marcuse's coalition is based upon the manifestation of the simple desire to renounce contemporary society, rather than upon some intellectual compatibility. The vanguard, therefore, ranges from ideological revolutionaries to self-proclaimed social exiles.

Of course, it is obvious enough that Marcuse's ideas concerning "liberation" do not espouse liberation, per se, but perceive liberation as an emancipation from an existing set of arrangements, in order that a new set of arrangements will prevail from which no further liberation is required. The crux of Marcuse's contentions finally turns on definitions of human needs. It is clear enough that Marcuse's conception of needs is markedly different from either a Marxist viewpoint or those identifiable with liberal democracy. But a new conception of needs rests, perforce, on a new conception of the nature of the person. Marcuse's underlying doctrine of the person, however, is finally quite as reductionistic as those he finds unacceptable. If man cannot live as a machine or as a status symbol or as a mindless consumer, it is also more than likely that he cannot exist solely on the basis of primal appetite. He certainly cannot long subsist on a diet of sheer protest or revolutionary stimulation. Can Marcuse's definitions provide the foundations for a society in some form of stasis, some enduring satisfactions beyond the temporary surcease of sublimation? That would seem a pivotal question.

PERSONAL CONSCIENCE AND SOCIAL
CONTROL

The social theory of the new radicalism is in one respect reminiscent of the thoughts of Rousseau: a problem exists regarding what appears to be, in one aspect, an endorsement of a type of individualism, of "doing your own thing," and yet with a parallel, if not over-riding, emphasis on virtually total social control. The writings of Paul Goodman, popular with the New Left, suggest this erratic shift of preference between a flamboyant, quasi-anarchistic individualism and a zeal for a centrally-conditioned "closed" society. Stokeley Carmichael, while addressing the Dialectics of Liberation Congress in London in 1967, observed, "I'm not a psychologist or a psychiatrist. I'm a political activist and I don't deal with the individual. I think it's a cop-out when people talk about the individual."

But the genesis of the new radicalism arose in part from the "identity crisis" of the present age, a fact acknowledged by many New Left commentators. The recovery of the Self is an important aspect of the new radicalism. Its response is not an original one: the Self is to be recovered by participation in a new mass social consciousness and political movement in which identity, the definition of the Self, will be formed by a *participation mystique*. Some critics have pointed out in this regard that such a viewpoint parallels another form of twentieth century radicalism: fascism. The word fascist is a common New Left term of opprobrium, but there are disquieting similarities between the emphasis of some new radicals on social control and the totalitarian convictions of fascism. To be more precise, there is, in the new radicalism, a yearning for the return to the reinforcements of communal identifications. This accounts for the tribalistic, even totemistic, quasi-mystical motifs in the New Left. There is genuine sensitivity in this reaction, yet it is often confused by a growing hostility in the New Left between a penchant for ideological puritanism and a romantic hedonism. This conflict is evident in Marcuse; it is manifest in the increasing fragmentation of the student Left.

There is also a new moralism in much of the thought of the new radicals. In part, this is a reaction to the moral indefiniteness of the century, an era of considerable ethical hypocrisy and cant. The ethical outlook of the New Left can be briefly described as a preference for moral absolutism without much enthusiasm for examining the problems of value mechanism or the ontological status of value. Its convictions are, again, not unlike those of Rousseau: a penetration into the realm of absolute value by subjective feeling. But the question arises as to whether such subjective feelings are generated by private introspection or by group feelings, especially those stimulated by a mood of social rebellion. The herd instincts of the new radicalism are very powerful, resulting in a striking uniformity of ideas, speech, behavior, and even dress. It may be, in a manner of speaking, an "easy" morality, however lofty the tone of the language that describes it, a morality of sententious abstractions in which subjective feelings, however generated, become uncritically transposed into ethical postulates. In any case, a characteristic of the new radicalism is to frame virtually all social and political controversy in the often angry language of moral absolutism, propelled by an indefatigable sense of moral superiority.

The rallying focus of the New Left is that revolution is at once inevitable and desirable. Just as the Marxists in the late nineteenth century argued over the question of the irreplaceability of violence as a feature of revolution, the new radicals debate the same topic. Attitudes range from a comprehensive endorsement of non-violence, even the abolition of social competition, to an admiration for deliberate terrorism. It is difficult to reconcile these points of view, even if both support the revolutionary ideal. It is hard to revere Gandhi and Guevara at the same time. Yet the techniques of massive non-violent demonstration and "civil disobedience" are never far from violence, even if such methods do not directly instigate it. In a sense, the concepts of civil disobedience practiced by Gandhi or Martin Luther King do rest on physical force, even if armed combat is not involved. The point to be made is that the New Left displays little faith in intellectual persuasion, preferring the instrumentalities of pressure, violent or non-violent. There is, indeed, a type of apocalyptical spirit in the new radicalism, a belief that a new order must be forged in the fire-bath of some ultimate and final confrontation—only in explicit descriptions do these radical visions differ, some manifestly sanguinary, others less physically destructive. Although David Thoreau is admired and much quoted by the new radicals, their conception of disobedience or protest is never as solitary as that proposed by the sometime resident of Walden Pond. For them, only mass protest and disobedience is seen as effective, because the issue is really not one of personal conscience, but of social control, a triumph that, allegedly, the future holds.

The emphasis on mass movements, violence, and the pre-chiliastic struggle in New Left thought represents yet another form of the rejection of the feasibility of rational solutions to cultural problems. The irrationality of much of twentieth century life can only be countered, the new radicalism proposes, by a more immediate and violent irrationalism. The "liberation" of which the radicals so enthusiastically speak is a liberation not only from the confines of circumstance, but a liberation from the restrictions of rationally-postulated thought, so as to give full vent to the otherwise inhibited passions. The history of political philosophy can be divided, in one way, between those who suspect the desirability of the free play of the passions and, conversely, those who see in human passion the culmination of wisdom and goodness. Contemporary radicalism is a current expression of this latter point of view, but one hedged by a fairly definitive conception of what these human passions are and what wisdom and goodness they are presumed to contain.

FOR ADDITIONAL READING

ABRAHAMSON, DAVID, *Our Violent Society*. New York: Funk & Wagnalls, 1970.

ARENDT, HANNAH, *On Revolution*. New York: Viking, 1963.

CARMICHAEL, S. and C. V. HAMILTON, *Black Power*. New York: Random House, 1967.

CLEAVER, ELDRIDGE, *Soul on Ice*. New York: McGraw-Hill, 1968.

FANON, FRANTZ, *The Wretched of the Earth* (trans. by Constance Farrington). New York: Grove Press, 1965.

GOODMAN, PAUL, *Growing Up Absurd: Problems of Youth in the Organized System*. New York: Random House, 1960.

GUEVARA, CHE, *Guerilla War*. New York: Monthly Review Press, 1961.

HABERMAS, JÜRGEN, *Toward a Rational Society: Student Protest, Science and Politics* (trans. by Jeremy Shapiro). Boston: Beacon Press, 1970 (orig. pub. 1968).

MARCUSE, HERBERT, *One-Dimensional Man*. Boston: Beacon Press, 1964.

MOORE, BARRINGTON, *The Social Origins of Dictatorship and Democracy*. Boston: Beacon Press, 1966.

WILLS, GARY, *The Second Civil War: Arming for Armageddon*. New York: Signet (New American Library), 1968.

WOLFF, R. P., *The Poverty of Liberalism*. Boston: Beacon Press, 1968.

TEN

Mortgaging the Hereafter

Futurism

Now, after having scanned the spectrum of twentieth century political philosophy, one rather elusive perspective remains to be examined. A result of the nineteenth-century emphasis upon explanations of the historical process was a good deal of conjecture regarding the future shapes of cultures. One can see this prophetic bent in Nietzsche, Dilthey, Spengler, and Arnold Toynbee, to name but a few. This form of *futuristic* speculation usually proceeded from one of two assumptions: (1) a belief in the inevitability of progress, or (2) the conviction that history followed some pattern resulting from the activity of decisive forces, variously described. Twentieth-century futurism appears to embrace different assumptions; there is an apocalyptic air about much of it, suggesting that the future holds some cataclysmic redirection of human destiny that will either be fortuitous or will present mankind with new and sweeping options or, alternatively, will pose a dire threat to survival, biologic or cultural. These reflections, consequently, are either extravagantly utopian or imply the coming of a new Dark Age or the actual extermination of the species.

One form of this utopianism proceeds from an unabashed admiration for the potentiality of technology. This technocratic enthusiasm goes far beyond a faith in the prospects of nuclear power or conquest of disease. It stresses the culturally redemptive capabilities of technological ingenuity. A particularly interesting example of this mode of thought is provided by the *communicationists* who see, in the accelerating improvements of the techniques of communication, a radical and beneficial transformation of the culture and even a new global cosmopolitanism that will usher in an era of peace and trans-cultural understanding. Marshall MacLuhan has announced that the "communications revolution" has made of the world a "global village." In his numerous works MacLuhan argues that the forms of communication—the media—created by sophisticated electronic innovation are decisively changing the manner in which we think. Our thought processes are no longer the product of written language or even discursive ideas, but are responses to the sensual evocations of electronic communication. MacLuhan views this situation with favor. This change in the mode of thought, he concludes, will presumably abolish old and anti-social prejudices, largely engrained by traditional intellectualism. A new era of social egalitarianism will result, employing immediate gratifications and cultural uniformities.

Not all share MacLuhan's somewhat neo-Pavlovian optimism regarding a new world order conditioned by electronic "inputs." MacLuhan's qualitative inferences seem unjustified, if only for the reason that it appears impossible to divorce the qualitative response from the quality of that which is communicated, the "medium" being, after all, only a means of transference, it is only as beneficial as are the motives and talents of those who operate it. No doubt, in another area, high-level computers are extremely useful devices, but they remain, at present, dependent on some initial human wisdom. The age of "robotry" is at hand, but, as yet, there seems no replacement for human judgment.

THE ECOLOGY MOVEMENT VS. THE TECHNOCRATS

This enthusiasm for the technological advance has not been universally shared, as is evidenced by the growth of what has been called the *ecology movement*. Although some who have become alarmed over damage to the physical environment have reacted with an expressed desire to return to more primitive lifestyles, by and large, these notions have not been typical of the new sensitivity to environmental problems. More common has been an attack upon the social effects of technology. The thrust of much anti-technological argument has been to question the deification of technological innovation as an end in itself, in contrast to appraising it in connection with real and potential benefits to people. Indeed, some *environmentalists* (not to be confused with this term as applied to certain neo-positivists) have asserted the need to use technological means to repair the damage wrought by technological irresponsibility.

The contemporary ecology movement divides itself into two broad categories: (1) those who see, in reckless technological exploitation, a critical disregard for the qualitative effects of technology; and (2) those who see in the ecology issue an opportunity to extend the broad assault upon capitalism and to buttress arguments in favor of public ownership and the abolition of a competitive economic system.

The technocrats are not vague about the exposition of their position, against which the environmentalists react so intensely. For illustration, Leland Hazard, in his article, "Challenges for Urban Policy" in *Values and the Future* by Baier and Rescher, projects this future vision:

> Downgraded by the computer and television will be: self-reliance, prowess and ability, freedom from interference, privacy, prudence, patriotism, and human dignity. Upgraded will be: physical well-being and comfort, economic security, friendship, intelligence, reasonableness and rationality, law and order, culture, novelty, equality and civil rights, social justice, peace, and internationalism. (p. 331)

Regardless of the competing claims of value (implied by Hazard's somewhat chaotic catalogue), some observers have less sanguine estimates of the social conditions produced by increasing technological development and urbanization. The ecological critics contend that uncontrolled and indiscriminate technology has not only brought the society to a state of biological crisis, but the changes brought about by this technology have created life patterns incompatible with human nature. There is an almost spiritualistic tenor in this criticism: the assumption that human nature requires the preservation of some minimal standard of environmental satisfaction, psychological and aesthetic, that demands the preservation of contact with nature, the solitude and refreshment provided by the maintenance of natural sanctuaries, within the concrete and steel artifacts of the technological age. There is an invocation of what D. H. Lawrence once called "cosmic piety." Such is the orientation, for illustration, of such organized bodies of conservationists as the Sierra Club.

The advocates of the technological advance make two fundamental arguments: (1) technological progress is inevitable in any case and (2) certain deprivations (presumably "privacy" or "human dignity") are reasonably to be borne in light of the advantages gained (presumably "physical well-being and comfort" or "economic security"). Implicit in the pro-technology position is the premise that because products of technological progress far outweigh the social sacrifices, men can be trained to accept and appreciate these compensations, suggesting, as well, that there exists no irrevocable natural human requirement that could be decisively abused by the lifestyles introduced by technological progress. If palpable human welfare in terms of health, productivity, comfort, and convenience can be realized by technological means, the technocrats maintain, the largely aesthetic deprivations occasioned by the modifications of the environment are trivial. How many people anyway, they ask, are really willing to jettison the advantages of an urbanized, industrialized way of life for the infrequent opportunity to "commune with nature"?

But the retort of the environmentalists is not only rendered in terms of the aesthetic or spiritualistic preferences of groups such as the Sierra Club. Significant numbers of American scientists and ecologists extend more concrete arguments, such as the work of

Barry Commoner, especially his book, *The Closing Circle*. The rebuttal is that rapacious technology has jeopardized the survival of the species, that the biological order is now seriously threatened by the inability or unwillingness of people to live in concert with the natural world around them. Moreover, some assert, human sanity will be endangered by the continued alienation of man from his roots and connections in nature. Paradoxically, this dispute between technocrats and environmentalists creates some highly unusual political stances. The technocrats, nominally associated with industrial and commercial interests, maintain that only technological progress can create economic and social justice—for example, the future of the "under-developed" peoples requires technology and industrialization. Conversely, the environmentalists, often associated in the popular mind with radical criticism of the society, press a distinctly conservative position, to wit, the necessity of conservation, opposition to change, and the recognition of nonmaterial values as primary.

Although the ecology issue often is articulated in terms devoid of philosophic substance, such as clean air versus industrial growth, fundamentally, the dispute strikes hard at the heart of the twentieth century dilemma: whether or not there exist elemental requirements for human social existence that must be recognized in the activity of social and political decision-making and planning.

A possible response to that vital question is put forward by an intellectual current distinctly different from the implicit utopianism of the technocrats or various futuristically-oriented theorists like Kenneth Boulding or Teilhard de Chardin. Coming into prominence has been a new anthropology resting primarily on the empirical investigation of animal behavior and its significance in understanding human behavior and social organization, both in an evolutionary and contemporary context. The core conception of this anthropology is provided by *ethology*, the study of animal behavior in terms of instinctual patterns of behavior. The pioneers in ethology have been Nicholas Tinbergen and Conrad Lorenz. Mention might be made of Tinbergen's *The Study of Instinct* and Lorenz's *On Aggression*.

The primary tenet of ethology is the rejection of the tabula rasa theory of mind—the concept of the mind as an "empty tablet" possessing no pre-experiential knowledge. On the contrary, the ethologists maintain that humans have innate, pre-experiential "wiring" that can be analyzed in biological terms; hence the revival, in social thought, of the theory of instinct. Ethology produced a variety of formulations regarding behavior as motivated and conditioned by "innate releasing mechanisms" (IRM), "imprinting," and other pre-experiential and subrational factors.

A number of contemporary biologists and anthropologists endeavored to translate these biological concepts gleaned from a study of animal behavior into more distinctly human terms, such as Desmond Morris, Robert Ardrey, Robert Bigelow, Lionel Tiger, and Robin Fox, to name a few. In addition, much research was undertaken regarding the similarities between the structures of animal and human societies, inferences drawn largely from the group behavior of primates, as with the observations of Solly Zuckerman, Irven DeVore, George Schaller, and Jane van Lawick-Goodall.

The primary anthropological conclusions drawn from a wide range of approaches appeared to be these: (1) man and his society were far more closely related to the animal world than was previously imagined; (2) human behavior is predominantly instinctual at base; (3) human behavior is primordially determined, but modified by evolution; (4) there are naturalistically-derived norms that could be applied to human society.

The full social implications of these theories are yet to be fully examined, especially in political terms, although some initial efforts are provided in the work of Donald Atwell Zoll. One of the more contentious precepts to emerge is the view that man is innately predacious and aggressive, recalling a similar though differently explained hypothesis of Freud. This argument has been specifically advanced by Robert Ardrey, under the influence of the theories of the paleontologist, Raymond Dart, and Robert Bigelow, a zoologist. This viewpoint and, indeed, the general ethological position has been sharply attacked by the American anthropologist, Ashley Montague, among others. It is supposed by Ardrey and others that the contemporary human is a descendant of a prehistorical "killer ape," retaining much of his ancestral aggressiveness.

The principal philosophical implications of the new anthropology, in the view of Zoll, is the stress placed upon the principles of *hierarchy* and *care-taking*. The import of this speculation appears to be that societies, including the human society, are invariably hierarchical in character and reflect a subordination of the individual member to group aims. These group aims include the survival of the society itself, the rearing of the young, and the defense against external threat.

This biologically-based anthropology has occasioned a new perspective on society, a revival of social organicism. It has considered society in terms of various "bonding" processes, in which conscious social options in regard to values and institutions are circumscribed by biological paradigms. Inferentially, then, present human societies can be appraised in terms of whether they fall within these naturalistic parameters, even in terms of such factors as over-crowding, disruptions of hierarchy, neglect of imprinting and care-taking, and the inhibition of fundamental needs. The idea of the aberrational social organization now appears feasible on the basis of a new criterion of social normality. Conceivably, this anthropological outlook could produce a canon of social necessities upon which subsequent social theory would have to be rationally constituted.

THE FUTURE: RADICALIZATION OF POLITICS

Two unmistakable factors emerge from the second half of the century that will probably decisively affect the climate for political philosophy. The first is the loosening of the hold of liberalism on the western democracies. The second is more abstruse, but nonetheless crucial: the disappearance of a viable sense of community and some preliminary and largely abortive attempts to recover it.

The liberalism that is currently under attack in the West is not the explicit tenet of classical liberalism, but the general post-Lockean political orientations that have undergirded political leadership in the democratic states. This liberal mood has consisted of a blend of ingredients: moderation, pluralism, equilibriumism, preeminence of the individual, belief in progress, and ethical relativism. There is considerable evidence to suppose that this tradition is withering away under the impact of cultural pressure and social agitation. To some extent, the demise of religion as an effective form of social influence is connected with this mounting critique of the liberal stewardship, the virtually unbroken continuity of liberal leadership for at least a century and a half. The declining potency of the liberal attitude tends, therefore, to encourage a volatile political atmosphere.

There can be scarce doubt that the remaining decades of the century will reveal a definite radicalization of politics, reflected in the supportive literature of that politics. Such a radicalization does not imply the domination of the new radicalism previously discussed, but rather a recasting of political issues and principles in new and more radical forms. In the vacuum created by the passing of liberalism, society will have to select from among numerous alternatives. Most of these alternatives will advocate striking reconstructions, political and social, of the culture. There will be, undoubtedly, a good deal of instability in this avowedly experimental predicament. The grave danger in this situation lies in the abandonment of a broadly rational approach to the postulation of political and social theory. In which case, the installation of an irrationalism could arise from the mood of intolerance that might result from a conflict between rival radicalisms, all embracing a belligerent moral absolutism. Ideology might, in fact, stamp out social philosophy, at least in the terms we have become accustomed.

Yet this process of radicalization is inevitable, if only for the reason that a new ethos must be forthcoming, as the liberal *Weltanschauung* becomes ossified and inadequate. The focus of this radical speculation will very likely center about the problem of community. The problem refers to the loss of satisfactions and reinforcements of communal life. The loss of identity in contemporary culture is traceable to a loss of those aspects of communal life productive of self-knowledge and awareness of the reciprocal obligations of social existence.

What is *community?* A community is a self-contained social organism in which a sense of belonging and of participation in group responsibilities exists. It need not be an isolated hamlet or commune; ideally, the state, the nation, is a community of a sort, although its size usually renders it more a collection of communities. The sense of community membership has been attacked both by the creation of mass forms of social organization and by the increasing egocentrism of the age.

Although the actuality of community may be largely obliterated, a virtually primordial need for communal participation perseveres. Contemporaneously, this sense of need manifests itself in frenetic efforts to compensate for the loss of community, by an attempt to create, spontaneously, substitute communities and institutions. But while the external forms of community change in the process of social evolution, all genuine communities display a central conceptualization of reciprocal responsibility and conduct. They project, in other words, a civic ethic.

The explicit civic ethics of various communities differ as a result of cultural and historical factors, but they also contain certain identical characteristics, the principal one being the entertainment of a civic ethic as an indispensable feature of social organization, plus the recognition and definition of legitimate authority, and a regard for the preservation of the social continuity.

We are passing through an era not unlike that of Greek society after the collapse of the Athenian ascendancy, in which our emphasis is almost exclusively upon the problem of the individual's moral predicament and survival. We ask the same question that was posed by the Arabic philosophers of the middle ages, "How is a good man to live in the evil city?" The difficulty in framing a satisfactory personal ethic under these conditions is the presumed unavailability of a civic ethic as a point of reference, to say nothing of the possible gratifications that follow from an awareness of, and subordination to, a social code that extends both security and freedom.

In short, the problem of the restoration of community is inevitably tied to the question of social ethics and both considerations affect the resolution of our choices regarding the more radical formulations of social values and goals. It can be said, however, that in analyzing the political and social literature of the late 1970s and '80s, we might well be advised to search for rational theories of community and its revival, for careful discussions of the civic ethic and, in general, for recommendations regarding future political order that discloses an enduring concern for rudimentary human needs.

THE GAP BETWEEN POLITICAL PRACTICE AND PHILOSOPHY

If one attempted to reduce the peregrinations of political philosophy in this century to one sentence, that proposition might be this: as the cultural life of the twentieth century became increasingly politicalized, political philosophy rushed to keep up and to provide a theoretical base for political activity. It is a fair estimate that, so far, it has failed. That discouraging judgment is made more disquieting if one adds to it the undeniable conclusion that the pace and intensity of political activity still increases, thus potentially widening the gap between practice and philosophy. Philosophy, after all, is some kind of rational enterprise, in contrast to the understandings of the heart or the stomach, estimable as these alternative understandings might be. Understanding of a cerebral type, whatever else it might be, is slow—in contrast, again, to the instantaneous revelations of the heart and the stomach. Thought probably has always been painful, from the days when Australopithecus or his equivalent decided to rely on something other than brute instinct. Likely mankind was forced to it out of desperation. In any case, the plaintive cry of the philosopher in the twentieth century might well be, "Stop the world, I want to get off!" But, alas, the whirling orb, propelling emotions, interests, events fails to slow down so he can get his bearings and, as a matter of fact, it speeds up—leaving everyone more than a little giddy.

The fact that cultural process accelerates and philosophy or rational thinking lags behind does not necessarily mean that civilization, as we know it, is in some irrevocable collision course with a fiery destiny. It has been fashionable in our times to use the metaphor of the "wave of the future" or similar imagery. Such language makes sense only if one is a died-in-the-wool historical determinist. We are not yet locked into some historical momentum that is impervious to our will. In a manner of speaking, we become too prone to accept the idea that reason is an anachronism or, at least, is a means too ponderous to cope with the stark reality of change and the formidable irrational forces that likely will parade across the concluding decades of the century. There are, in fact, two quite reliable methods of retarding this drift toward believing in the futility of reason. The first involves not halting the cultural processes, but "culling out," as it were, those contributions to the acceleration of the process that do not arise from normative concern, but rather from a common zest for innovation and novelty. Our culture increasingly reminds one of the phenomenon of hotel building at Miami Beach. There, perfectly useable and attractive hotels are demolished and new ones constructed in their place, for no other reason than the supposition that prospective customers will flock to the new structures because they are new.

The second method requires the abandonment of a dichotomy between political philosophy (as both a rational and a reasonably aloof enterprise) and political decision-making (presumably pragmatic and relevant). Our culture has seen a widening chasm between the philosopher and the politician, far exceeding the differences existent in the nineteenth century. It would seem truly quaint, today, for us to suggest the desirability of our political leaders possessing a "philosophy" of politics, at least beyond the enunciation of the slogans of mass appeal. Unless we are able to reconcile the bases upon which we make philosophical judgments with those upon which we make more or less day-to-day political judgments, we are very apt to be spun along in the undercurrent of social pressures, without being able to constrain or direct them.

Nor can our judgments about how we choose to live be considered only within the relatively narrow confines of so-called political "theory." The twentieth century is notable for marking the ultimate fruition of a long-standing development in western thought: the separation of the idea of virtue into two exclusive parts—*political* virtue and *personal* virtue. In other words, our concepts of political "good" and "bad" are strikingly different from the definitions of "good" and "bad" we commonly use in the nonpolitical sphere. This separation provides a discrete momentum for political phenomena and often excludes it from the judgmental criteria, particularly moral ones, that we would ordinarily apply.

An important function of political philosophy in the waning years of the century will be, then, to separate the normative element in change from the purely novel, to bring together the philosophical and the political discourse (and, perhaps, even the vocations themselves) and to establish a common moral base for both political and general behavior.

Such an undertaking is hardly a modest one. On the contrary, it is an expansive task and one unfamiliar to many whose conception of the vocation of the social philosopher is far less comprehensive and imperative. It requires one to take a deep breath and take the plunge into murky waters. The emerging shape of the culture places a new and insistent emphasis on Aristotle's ancient contention that *political* referred to all aspects of man's relations in society. As the political touches us, increasingly, in every phase of our existence, it becomes necessary to widen the scope of political philosophy to adequately encompass this range. But the extension of that range of interests and competency cannot mean a dilution of the rational precision with which we deal with political and social questions. We merely increase the strain upon the resources of the political philosopher. His ability to cope with these enhanced responsibilities will depend upon two factors: the quality of his personal resolve and the quality of his education. But education, granted some availability of resources, is finally an intimate, self-acquired experience, and it defies the programmatic devices of the indoctrinator.

Our fate as a culture, indeed, as a species, yet hangs upon this essentially private passion, this strange urgent demand to know, this ability to "listen with the third ear." Like any historical era, this century is replete with shame and pride, stupidity and creation and, invariably, with promise—a promise to be redeemed, as always, by the spirit of the human intellect.

FOR ADDITIONAL READING

BAIER, K. and N. RESCHLER, eds., *Values and the Future.* New York: Free Press, 1969.

BIGELOW, ROBERT, *The Dawn Warriors: Man's Evolution Toward Peace.* Boston: Little, Brown, 1969.

BOGUSLAW, R., *The New Utopians: A Study of System Design and Social Change*. Englewood Cliffs, N.J.: Prentice-Hall, 1965.

BOULDING, KENNETH, *The Meaning of the Twentieth Century: The Great Transition*. New York: Harper & Row, 1964.

COMMONER, BARRY, *The Closing Circle: Nature, Man and Technology*. New York: Knopf, 1971.

ELLUL, JACQUES, *The Technological Society* (trans. by John Wilkinson). New York: Knopf, 1964.

HEILBRONER, R. L., *The Future as History*. New York: Harper, 1960.

HUXLEY, ALDOUS, *The Politics of Ecology: The Question of Survival*. Santa Barbara: Center for the Study of Democratic Institutions, 1963.

McLUHAN, H. M. and Q. FIORE, *War and Peace in the Global Village*. New York: McGraw-Hill, 1968.

MORRIS, DESMOND, *The Human Zoo*. New York: McGraw-Hill, 1969.

SIMON, HERBERT, *The Shape of Automation*. New York: Harper & Row, 1965.

TIGER, L. and R. FOX, *The Imperial Animal*. New York: Holt, Rinehart & Winston, 1971.

Glossary

AXIOLOGY.   The study of the theory of value.

CAUSAL DETERMINISM.   Belief in the reliability and uniformity of the cause and effect relationship in which cause consistently determines effect.

CAUSALITY.   The relationship of cause and effect.

EMPIRICISM.   A general belief in the premise that experience is the primary or only source or mode of knowledge.

EPISTEMOLOGY.   The branch of philosophical study concerned with the investigation of the problem of knowledge.

ESCHATOLOGY.   Study and discourse regarding the final ends of things, particularly man.

IRRATIONALISM.   The general conviction that truth or understanding is neither exclusively nor predominantly conveyed by rational processes.

METAPHYSICS.   The branch of philosophy concerned with the consideration of first principles, of ultimate, irreducible questions of greatest generality.

NATURALISM.   The general viewpoint that reality can be adequately accounted for within the confines of nature.

NIHILISM.   The denial of either objective truth or reality; more popularly, a disbelief in moral principles or in the significance of human life.

NOMINALISM.   The denial of the objective existence of universals or essences.

ONTOLOGY.   The branch of philosophy concerned with the analysis of Being or reality.

PANPSYCHISM.   The view that reality, the elemental categories of nature, correspond to psychic activity.

PHYSICALISM.   Either the reduction of all definitions of reality to physical substances or the contention that scientific terminology is directly related to observable physical properties.

QUIETISM.   The advocacy of resignation, withdrawal, subjective contemplation, and a generally ascetic perspective.

SUBJECTIVISM.   The assertion that all knowledge ends with the experiences of the individual self.

TABULA RASA.   Literally, an "empty slate"; a reference to the mind as containing no pre-experiential content.

TELEOLOGY.   The study of the evidences of the existence of purpose or design in the universe.

THEOLOGY.   The study of the nature of God and of God's relationship to the world of immediate reality.

Index

Gentile, Giovanni, 41, 42, 43
Gide, Andre, 7
Gilson, Etienne, 148, 149
Gobineau, Joseph de, 37, 42
Goethe, Johann Wolfgang von, 119, 129
Goldwater, Barry, 123
Goodall, Jane van Lawick, 172
Goodman, Paul, 163
Grant, Madison, 7, 121, 127
Great Britain, 38, 50, 68, 86
Greece, 49
Guevara, Che, 153, 165

H

Hall, G. Stanley, 21
Hallowell, John, 94
Hart, H. L. A., 86
Hartmann, Nicolai, 32, 33, 34, 121
Hawthorne, Nathaniel, 119
Hayden, Tom, 157
Hayek, Frederic, 133
Hazard, Leland, 169
Hegel, Georg, 14, 37, 42, 43, 159
Hegelianism, 14, 41, 137
Heidegger, Martin, 137
Herberg, Will, 123
Herder, Johann von, 42, 43
Hindenburg, Paul von, 39
Hitler, Adolf, 39, 42, 44, 49, 55
Hobbes, Thomas, 37, 92, 93
Hocking, William, 121
Hogg, Quinton, 129
Holder, Eric, 11
Holland, 68
Hospers, John, 133
Human Nature in Politics (Wallas), 70
Humanism, 10, 149
Hume, David, 71, 72, 82, 85, 92
Hungary, 66
Husserl, Edmund, 120

I

Id, 23-24, 27
Idea of the Christian Community, The (Eliot), 122
Idealism, 14-15, 34, 41

Ideology and Utopia (Mannheim), 78
Imperialism, 56-57, 156
India, 69
Individualism, 15, 27, 28, 31-32, 83, 95, 105-107, 123, 133
Industrial Revolution, 73, 118, 119, 154
Instrumentalism, 96
Interpretation of Dreams, The (Freud), 21
Introductory Lectures on Psychoanalysis (Freud), 22
Irrationalism, 4, 41, 43, 45, 78, 153, 174
Israel, 68
Italy, 41, 49, 68

J

James, William, 22, 40, 79, 96, 108
Japan, 39, 42, 44, 49
Jaspers, Karl, 137, 138-40, 148
Jefferson, Thomas, 130
Jouvenel, Bertrand de, 9, 123
Jung, Carl Gustav, 19, 21, 25, 28, 31, 34, 74, 128

K

Kant, Immanuel, 48, 71, 138
Kariel, Henry, 99, 110-11, 112, 115
Kelsen, Hans, 82
Kent, Chancellor, 123
Khrushchev, Nikita, 62
Kierkegaard, Søren, 137, 138
King, Martin Luther, 153, 165
Kirk, Russell, 122, 124

L

Labour Party, British, 68
Laissez-faire, 123, 133
Language, Truth and Logic (Ayers), 88
Language philosophy, 84-87
Laslett, Peter, 85
Lasswell, Harold, 81, 99, 103-5, 111
Lawrence, D. H., 128, 170
Laws (Plato), 45